ON THE WORSHIP OF GOD

John Owen

Vintage Puritan Series
GLH Publishing

Originally Titled *A Brief Instruction in the Worship of God and Discipline of the Churches of the New Testament.*
Sourced from *The Works of John Owen*. Vol. XV.
Edited by William Goold. T. & T. Clark, London, 1862.

ISBN:
Paperback 978-1-948648-91-2

Sign up for updates from GLH Publishing using the link below and receive a free ebook.
http://eepurl.com/gj9V19

CONTENTS

Prefatory Note. 1

A Short Catechism with an Explication Upon
the Same. 4

Prefatory Note.

The following Catechism explains the constitution and ordinances of a Christian Church, and the duties incumbent on its office-bearers and members. When it was first published, in 1667, the names of the author and of the printer were withheld, and no intimation even was given of the place in which it was printed, lest danger should be incurred by the publication of a work advocating a form of polity at variance with the ecclesiastical system which the Court was at that time striving to render, as far as possible, universal in England. Dissenting congregations were, however, springing up in different parts of the country, and for the guidance of the Independents the Catechism was particularly useful. It was so much appreciated, that in the same year in which it first appeared, a second edition, with some slight differences and emendations, was published; and hence certain discrepancies between the following version of it and the one which is given in Russell's edition of our author's works, printed from the first edition of the Catechism.

It came to be known as the "Independents' Catechism," and an angry attack was made upon it, in 1669, by Benjamin Camfield, rector of Whitby, in Derbyshire, in an octavo volume of 347 pages, entitled "A Serious Examination of the Independents' Catechism, and therein of the Chief Principles of Nonconformity to, and Separation from, the Church of England." The Catechism, in the estimation of the rector, was "the sink of all nonconforming and separating principles;" and he takes Owen to task for inconsistency in holding the Scriptures to be a sufficient rule of faith and duty. An attack conducted in this spirit only bespeaks the influence which this Catechism was beginning to exert in diffusing the principles and consolidating the interests of the denomination to which its author belonged. It was the occasion of another attack upon Owen, in the shape of a frivolous and bitter pamphlet with the title, "A Letter to a Friend concerning some of Dr Owen's Principles and Practices," etc., 1670. A copy of the Catechism had been sent by the "Friend" to the anonymous author of the pamphlet, who forthwith assailed Owen in a strain of pointless invective. The first charge against him is, that when vice-chancellor at Oxford, he had discountenanced some invidious distinctions in the dress of the members of the university, — "those *habits* and *formalities* by which persons of distinct qualities and degrees were distinguished in that school of learning." It was an offence, too, that "when he was brought into Westminster Hall for his witness against Mr Dutton, he refused to kiss the book, and professed it to be against his conscience to swear with any other ceremony than with eyes and hands lifted up to heaven." The pamphlet closes with "An Independent Catechism," in which the views of our author are caricatured in a style that is intended to be witty.

Certain principles laid down in Owen's Catechism, in regard to the ruling elder for example, are thought to bear some traces of affinity with Presbyterianism. Encouraged especially by the doctrine taught in it, that the elders, not the body of the church, are the primary subjects of office-power, Baxter wrote to Owen a long document of "theses," as the basis of a union between Independents and Presbyterians. The reply of the latter will be found in the Appendix to his "Life," vol. I. p cxix. "I am still a well-wisher to these mathematics," was his remark, when he finally returned the theses to their author; and "this," says Baxter, "was the issue of my third attempt for union with the Independents." There might be ground for supposing that, on terms suggested by the Catechism, a coalition might be effected between the two denominations; and Owen himself, in a subsequent work (see p. 433 of this volume), indicated circumstances in which they could not have been in separation from each other without blame. Superior, however, in practical sagacity to his correspondent, he might see difficulties where Baxter saw none, or might feel that a formula of abstract theses was a waste of ingenuity, so long as the mutual confidence was lacking, which alone could affix upon the union the seal of permanence. Too often the victim of his own ardour and acumen, Baxter was prone to believe that the difficulty of adjusting the wayward eddies of human feeling and opinion into one smooth and onward current, should yield at once to the same treatment as would suffice to work a problem or frame a syllogism. The consummation for which he sincerely panted, — the outward unity of the church under one polity, — seems as yet reserved in providence to grace distant and happier times. — ED.

A Short Catechism with an Explication Upon the Same.

Ques. 1 *What doth God require of us in our dependence on him, that he may be glorified by us, and we accepted with him?*

Ans. That we ªworship him ᵇin and by the ways of his own appointment.—ªMatt. iv. 10; Rev. xiv. 7; Deut. vi. 13, x. 20.—ᵇLev. x. 1–3; Exod. xxiv. 3; Gen. xviii. 19; Josh. xxiii. 6–8; Zech. xiv. 16.

Explication. — By the worship of God inquired after, not that which is *natural* or *moral*, which is required in the first commandment, is intended. Such is our faith and confidence in him, our fear of him, our subjection of soul and conscience unto him, as the great sovereign Lord, First Cause, Last End, Judge, and Rewarder of all men; the law whereof was originally written in the heart of man, and hath been variously improved and directed by new revelations and institutions. And this worship is called *natural* upon a double account:—

First, Because it depends on the *nature of God*, a due perception and understanding whereof makes all this worship indispensably necessary: for none can know God but it is his duty to "glorify him as God," — that is, to believe in him, love him, trust him, and call upon him; which are all therefore cursed that do not, Ps. lxxix. 6; 2 Thess. i. 8.

And, secondly, Because it was in the principle

of it created with the *nature of man*, as that which suited, directed, and enabled him to answer the law of his creation, requiring this obedience of him in his dependence on God. And this worship is invariable: but it concerneth those outward ways and means whereby God hath appointed that faith, and love, and fear of him to be exercised and expressed unto his glory. And this kind of worship, though it depend not upon the nature of God, but upon his free and arbitrary disposal, and so was of old liable unto alterations, yet God did ever strictly require in the several states and conditions that his church hath gone through in the world. And this is that which most commonly in the Scripture is called by the name of "The worship of God," as that whereby all the acceptable actings of the souls of men towards him are expressed, and the only way of owning and acknowledging him in the world, as also of entertaining a visible intercourse with him. This, therefore, he calls for, and requires indispensably of all that draw nigh to him, and that because he is "the LORD our God," Rev. xiv. 6, 7; Matt. iv. 10; Deut. x. 12, 13. For his observance hereof doth he so approve of Abraham, Gen. xviii. 19; and sets it down as an everlasting law unto all others, that in a holy observation thereof "he will be sanctified in them that come nigh him," Lev. x. 1–3. His commands, also, concerning it are multiplied in the Scripture, with the approbation of all those that attend unto them. We may not think to find acceptance with God, or to inherit the promises, if, supposing ourselves to adhere unto him in worship internal and natural, we neglect that which is external and of his free appointment: for besides that we renounce thereby our inward dependence on him also, in not observing his commands, as Adam did in transgressing an institution, we become wholly useless unto all the ends of his glory in the world; which is not the way to come to an enjoyment of him. Neither do we only express and profess our inward *moral-natural worship* of God hereby, by which means it becomes the principal way and instrument of faith and trust exerting themselves in our obedience, but also it is a most effectual help and assistance unto the principle of that natural worship, strengthening the *habit* of it, and exciting it unto all suitable *actings*, unto its increase and growth.

Q. 2 *By what means do we come to know that God will thus be worshipped?*

A. That God is to be worshipped, and that according to his own will and appointment, is a ªprincipal branch of the law of our creation written in our hearts, the ᵇsense whereof is renewed in the second commandment; but the ways and means of that worship depend merely on God's ᶜsovereign pleasure and institution.—ªRom. i. 21, ii. 14, 15; Acts xiv. 16, 17, xvii. 23–31.—ᵇExod. xx. 4–6.—ᶜJer. vii. 31; Exod. xxv. 40; Heb. iii. 1–6; John i. 18.

EXPLICATION. — These two things all men saw by nature:—

First, That God, however they mistook in their apprehensions of him, would be, and was to be, worshipped with some *outward solemn* worship; so that although some are reported to have even cast off all knowledge and sense of a Divine Being, yet never any were heard of that came to an acknowledgment of any God, true or false, but they all consented that he was constantly and solemnly to be worshipped, and that not only by *individual persons*, but by *societies* together; that so they might own and honour him whom they took for their God. And thus far outward worship is required in the first commandment, — namely, that the inward be exercised and expressed. When we take God for our God, we take him to worship him, Deut. x. 12, 13. Other thoughts, — namely, of inward worship without outward expression, at all or any time, or in any way, — are but a covert unto atheism. And, —

Secondly, This also they were led to an apprehension of by the same light whereby they are "a law unto themselves," Rom. ii. 14, that God would be worshipped in the *way* and by the means that he himself appointed and approved: whence none among the heathen themselves undertook to appoint ways and ceremonies of worship, but still they pretended to derive the knowledge of them from the *gods themselves*; of whom they reckoned that every one would be worshipped in his own way. And because, notwithstanding this pretence, being left of God and deluded of Satan, they did invent false and foolish ways of worship, not only not appointed of God, but such as were unsuited unto those *inbred notions* which they had of his nature and excellencies, the apostle convinces and disproves them, as men acting against *the light of nature* and principles of reason, Rom. i. 20, 21, they might have seen that in their idolatry they answered not their own inbred conceptions of the divine power and Godhead, so as to "glorify him as God;" and in the like manner doth he argue at large, Acts xvii. 22–31. But beyond this the inbred light of nature could not conduct any of the sons of men; this alone is contained in the first precept. That God was to be worshipped they knew, and that he was to be worshipped by ways and means of his own appointment they knew; but what those means were they knew not. These always depended on God's sovereign will and pleasure, and he made them known to whom he pleased, Ps. cxlvii. 19, 20. And although some of the ways which he doth appoint may seem to have a great compliance in them unto the light of nature, yet in his worship he accepts them not on that account, but merely on that of his own institution; and this as he hath declared his will about in the second commandment, so he hath severely forbidden the *addition* of our own inventions unto what he hath appointed, sending us for instruction unto Him alone whom he hath endowed with *sovereign authority* to reveal his will and ordain his worship, John i. 18; Matt. xvii. 5; 1 Chron. xvi. 7.

Q. 3 *How, then, are these ways and means of the worship of God made known unto us?*

A. In and by the written word only, which contains a full and perfect revelation of the will of God as to his whole worship and all the concernments of it.—John v. 39; Isa. viii. 20; Luke xvi. 29; 2 Tim. iii. 15–17; 2 Pet. i. 19; Deut. iv. 2, xii. 32; Josh. i. 7; Prov. xxx. 6; Rev. xxii. 18, 19; Isa. xxix. 13, 14.

EXPLICATION. — The *end* wherefore God granted his word unto the church was, that thereby it might be instructed in his mind and will as to what concerns the worship and obedience that he requireth of us, and which is accepted with him. This the whole Scripture itself everywhere declares and speaks out unto all that do receive it; as 2 Tim. iii. 15–17, with the residue of the testimonies above recited, do declare. It supposeth, it declareth, that of ourselves we are ignorant how God is, how he ought to be, worshipped, Isa. viii. 20.

Moreover, it manifests him to be a "jealous God," exercising that holy property of his nature in an especial manner about his worship, rejecting and despising every thing that is not according to his will, that is not of his institution, Exod. xx. 4–6.

That we may know what is so, he hath made a revelation of his mind and will in his *written* word, — that is, the Scripture. And to the end that we might expect instruction from thence alone in his worship, and act therein accordingly, —

First, *He sends us and directs us thereunto* expressly for that purpose, Isa. viii. 20; Luke xvi. 29; John v. 39; and not once intimates in the least any other way or means of instruction unto that end.

Secondly, He frequently affirms that it is sufficient, able, and perfect to guide us therein, 2 Tim. iii. 15–17; 2 Pet. i. 19; Ps. xix. 7–9. And whereas he hath expressly given it unto us for that end, if there be any want or defect therein it must arise from hence, that either God would not or could not give unto us a perfect revelation of his will; neither of which can be imagined.

Thirdly, He hath commanded us to observe all whatsoever he hath appointed therein, and not to make any addition thereunto, Josh. i. 7; Deut. iv. 2, xii. 32; Prov. xxx. 6; Rev. xxii. 18, 19. And, —

Fourthly, Peculiarly interdicted us the use of any such things as are of the institution or appointment of men, Isa. xxix. 13, 14. So that from the Scriptures alone are we to learn what is accepted with God in his worship.

Q. 4 *Have these ways and means been always the same from the beginning?*

A. No; but God hath altered and changed them at sundry seasons, according to the counsel of his own will, so as he saw necessary for his own glory and the edification of his church.—Gen. ii. 16, 17, xvii. 10, 11; Exod. xii. 3–24, xx., xxv. 9; Heb. i. 1, 2, ix. 10–12.

EXPLICATION. — The *external* worship whereof we speak being, as was showed before, not natural or moral, arising necessarily from the dependence of the rational creature on God as its first cause, chiefest good, last end, and sovereign Lord, but proceeding from the mere will and pleasure of God, determining how he will be honoured and glorified in the world, was always alterable by him by whom it was appointed. And whereas, ever since the entrance of sin into the world, God had always respect unto the promise of the Lord Christ and his mediation, in whom alone he will be glorified, and faith in whom he aimed to begin and increase in all his worship, he hath suited his institutions of the means thereof to that dispensation of light and knowledge of him which he was pleased at any time to grant. Thus, immediately after the giving of the *promise*, he appointed *sacrifices* for the great means of his worship; as to glorify himself expressly by men's offering unto him of the principal good things which he had given them, so to instruct them in the faith, and confirm them in the expectation of *the great sacrifice* for sin that was to be offered by the promised seed, Gen. iv. 3, 4; Heb. xi. 4. These were the first instituted worship of God in the world after the entrance of sin. Hereunto he nextly added *circumcision*, as an express sign of the covenant, with the grace of it, which he called Abraham and his seed unto by Jesus Christ, Gen. xvii. 10, 11. And to the same general end and purpose he afterwards superadded the *passover*, with its attendant institutions, Exod. xii. 3–24; and then the whole law of institutions contained in ordinances, by the ministry of angels on mount Sinai, Exod. xx. So by sundry degrees he built up that fabric of his *outward worship*, which was suited, in his infinite wisdom, unto his own glory and the edification of his church, until the exhibition of the promised seed, or the coming of Christ in the flesh, and the accomplishment of the work of his mediation, Heb. i. 1, 2: for unto that season were those ordinances to serve, and no longer, chap. ix. 10–12, and then were they removed by the same authority whereby they were instituted and appointed, Col. ii. 14, 18–20. So that though God would never allow that men upon what pretence soever, should make any alteration in the worship appointed by him, by adding unto it anything of their own, or omitting aught that he had commanded, either in matter or manner, notwithstanding that he knew that it was to abide but for a season, but commanded all men straitly to attend to the observation of it whilst it was by him continued in force, Mal. iv. 4; yet he always reserved unto himself the sovereign power of altering, changing, or utterly abolishing it at his own pleasure: which authority he exerted in the gospel as to all the mere institutions of the Old Testament. Whilst they continued he enforced them with *moral* reasons, [such] as his own holiness and authority. But those reasons prove not any of those institutions to be *moral*, unless they ensue upon those reasons alone, and are nowhere else commanded; for being once instituted and commanded, they are to be enforced with moral considerations, taken from the nature of God and our duty in reference unto his authority. So saith he, "Thou shalt reverence my sanctuary, I am the LORD;" which no more proves that a moral duty than that enjoined upon the same foundation, Lev. xi. 44, "I am the LORD your God: ye shall therefore sanctify yourselves, and ye shall be holy; for I am holy: neither shall ye defile yourselves with any manner of creeping thing that creepeth upon the earth." Not defiling ourselves with the touching or eating of creeping things is now no moral duty since the institution is ceased, although it be enforced by many moral considerations.

Q. 5 *Is there any farther alteration to be expected in or of those institutions and ordinances of worship which are revealed and appointed in the gospel?*

A. No; the last complete revelation of the will of God being made by the Son, who is Lord of all, his commands and institutions are to be observed inviolably unto the end of the world, without alteration, diminution, or addition.—Heb. i. 1, 2, x. 25–27; Matt. xxviii. 20; 1 Cor. xi. 26; 1 Tim. vi. 14.

EXPLICATION. — It was showed before that all the institutions of the Old Testament had respect unto the coming of Christ in the flesh, who was "the end of the law," Rom. x. 4; and thereupon they were subject to alteration and abolition upon a twofold account:—

1. Because that which they were appointed principally to instruct the church in, and to direct it unto the expectation of, was, upon his coming, accomplished and fulfilled; so that their end was absolutely taken away, and they could no more truly teach the mind and will of God, for they would still direct unto that which was to come, after it was past and accomplished. And this is that which the apostle Paul so variously proves and fully confirms in his Epistle to the Hebrews, especially in the seventh, eighth, ninth, and tenth chapters.

2. The Lord Christ, during their continuance, was to come as the Lord over his whole house, with more full and ample authority than any of those whom God had employed in the institution of his ordinances of old were intrusted withal: Heb. i. 1–3, "He spake in time past by the prophets," but now "by his Son, whom he hath appointed heir of all." Chap. iii. 6, "Christ as a son over his own house; whose house are we." And, therefore, they were all to be at his disposal, to confirm or remove, as he saw reason and occasion. And this he did, — (1.) *Virtually*, in the sacrifice of himself, or the blood of his cross, fulfilling and finishing of them all, John xix. 30; "breaking down the middle wall of partition; abolishing in his flesh the enmity, even the law of commandments contained in ordinances;" "blotting out the hand-writing of ordinances," he "took it out of the way, nailing it to his cross," Eph. ii. 14, 15; Col. ii. 14. (2.) *Authoritatively*, by his Spirit in the apostles, and the doctrine of the gospel preached by them: Acts xv. 10, 11, "Now therefore why tempt ye God, to put a yoke upon the neck of the disciples, which neither our fathers nor we were able to bear? But we believe that through the grace of the Lord Jesus Christ we shall be saved, even as they." Gal. iii. 24, 25, "Wherefore the law was our schoolmaster to bring us unto Christ, that we might be justified by faith. But after that faith is come, we are no longer under a schoolmaster." Chap. v. 1–4. And, (3.) *Eventually* or providentially, when he caused sacrifice and offering to cease, by the prince of the people, that came with an army making desolate, to destroy both city and sanctuary, Dan. ix. 26, 27, according to his prediction, Matt. xxiv. 2. But now, under the New Testament, the worship that is ap-

pointed in the gospel is founded in and built upon what is already past and accomplished, — namely, the death and life of Jesus Christ, with the sacrifice and atonement for sin made thereby, 1 Cor. xi. 23–26; which can never be again performed; neither is there any thing else to the same purpose either needful or possible, Heb. x. 26. So that there is not any ground left for any new institution of worship, or any alteration in those that are already instituted. Nor, —

Secondly, Can any one be expected to come from God with a greater and more full authority for the revelation of his mind than that wherewith his only Son was accompanied; which yet must be, if any alterations were to be made in the appointments of worship that he hath instituted in the gospel.

For no inferior nor an equal authority can abolish or alter that which is already appointed, so as to give satisfaction unto the consciences of men in obedience unto such alterations. And, therefore, because there arose not a prophet like unto Moses under the Old Testament, there could be no alteration made in his institutions, but the church was bound severely to observe them all until the coming of Christ: Mal. iv. 4, "Remember ye the law of Moses my servant, which I commanded unto him in Horeb for all Israel, with the statutes and judgments;" and that because "there arose not a prophet afterwards in Israel like unto Moses, whom the Lord knew face to face," Deut. xxxiv. 10. And our apostle, to prove the right of Christ to alter the ordinances of the law, lays his foundation in manifesting that he was above the angels: Heb. i. 4, "Being made so much better than the angels, as he hath by inheritance obtained a more excellent name than they;" and that because the law was given by the ministry of angels, chap. ii. 2; — and so also that he was greater than Moses, chap. 3:3, 5, "For this man was counted worthy of more glory than Moses, inasmuch as he who hath builded the house hath more honour than the house. Moses verily was faithful in all his house, as a servant, but Christ as a son over his own house;" because Moses was the lawgiver, and the mediator between God and man in the giving of the law. Now, if this be the sole foundation and warrant of the alteration made of Mosaical ordinances by Christ, — namely, that he was greater and exalted above all those whose ministry was used in the dispensation of the law, — unless some can be thought to be greater, and exalted in authority above the Son of God, there can be no alteration expected in the institutions of the gospel.

Q. 6 *May not such an estate of faith and perfection in obedience be attained in this life, as wherein believers may be freed from all obligation unto the observation of gospel institutions?*

A. No; for the ordinances and institutions of the gospel being inseparably annexed unto the evangelical administration of the covenant of grace, they may not be left unobserved, disused, or omitted, whilst we are to walk before God in that covenant, without contempt of the covenant itself, as also of the wisdom and authority of Jesus Christ.—Heb. iii. 3–6; Rom. vi. 3–6; Luke xxii. 19, 20; 1 Cor. xi. 23–26; Heb. x. 25; Rev. ii. 5, iii. 3.

EXPLICATION. — All our faith, all our obedience in this life, whatever may be obtained or attained unto therein, it all belongs unto our walking with God in the covenant of grace, wherein God dwells with men, and they are his people, and God himself is with them to be their God. Other ways of communion with him, of obedience unto him, of enjoyment of him, on this side heaven and glory, he hath not appointed nor revealed. Now, this is the covenant that God hath made with his people, "That he will put his laws into their mind, and write them in their hearts, and will be to them a God, and they shall be to him a people; and he will be merciful to their unrighteousness, and their sins and their iniquities will he remember no more," Heb. viii. 9–12. And whatever men attain unto, it is by virtue of the grace of that covenant; nor is there any grace promised in the covenant to lead men in this life, or to give them up into a state of perfection, short of glory. Unto this covenant are the institutions of gospel-worship annexed, and unto that administration of it which is granted unto the church upon the coming and death of Christ. Without a renunciation and relinquishment of that covenant and the grace of it, these institutions cannot be omitted or deserted. If men suppose that they have attained to an estate wherein they need neither the grace of God, nor the mercy of God, nor the blood of Christ, nor the Spirit of Christ, it is not much material what they think of the ordinances of worship. Their pride and folly, without that mercy which is taught, promised, and exhibited in those ordinances, will speedily be their ruin. Besides, the Lord Christ is the absolute Lord "over his own house," Heb. iii. 3–6; and he hath given out the laws whereby he will have it guided and ruled whilst it is in this world. In and by these laws are his ordinances of worship established. For any persons, on what pretence soever, to plead an exemption from the obligation of those laws, it is nothing but to cast off the lordship and dominion of Christ himself. And yet farther to secure our obedience in this matter, he hath expressly commanded the continuance of them until his coming unto judgment, as in the places above quoted will appear.

Q. 7 *What are the chief things that we ought to aim at in our observation of the institutions of Christ in the gospel?*

A. ªTo sanctify the name of God; ᵇto own and avow our professed subjection to the Lord Jesus Christ; ᶜto build up ourselves in our most holy faith; and, ᵈto testify and confirm our mutual love, as we are believers.—ªLev. x. 3; Heb. xii. 28, 29.—ᵇDeut. xxvi. 17; Josh. xxiv. 22; 2 Cor. viii. 5. ᶜEph. iv. 11–16; Jude 20.—ᵈ1 Cor. x. 16, 17.

EXPLICATION. — That we may profitably and comfortably, unto the glory of God and our own edification, be exercised in the observation of the institutions and worship of God, we are always to consider what are the *ends* for which God hath appointed them and commanded our attendance unto them, that so our observance of them may be the obedience of faith. For, what end soever God hath appointed them unto, for that end are they useful and effectual, and to no other. If we come to them for any other end, if we use them for any other purpose or with any other design, if we look for any thing in them or by them, but what God hath appointed them to communicate unto us, we dishonour God and deceive our own souls. This we ought diligently to inquire into, to know not only *what* God requires of us, but *wherefore* also he requires it, and what he aims at therein; some of the principal things whereof are enumerated in this answer. And it is well known how horribly many of the institutions of the gospel have been by some (especially the Papists) abused, by a neglect of the ends of God in them, and imposing new ends of their own upon them, unto superstition and idolatry. Grace is ascribed unto the *outward observance* of them, whereas all grace is of the promise, and the promise in the covenant is given only to the faith of the right observers. The elements in the sacrament of the eucharist are turned into a god, first worshipped and then devoured, with many the like abominations.

Q. 8 *How may we sanctify the name of God in the use of gospel institutions?*

A. [a]By a holy reverence of his sovereign authority appointing of them; [b]a holy regard unto his special presence in them; [c]faith in his promises annexed to them; [d]delight in his will, wisdom, love, and grace, manifested in them; [e]constancy and perseverance in obedience unto him in their due observation.—[a]Lev. x. 3; Mal. i. 6; Rom. iv. 11; Exod. xx. 6; James iv. 12.—[b]Matt. xxviii. 20; Isa. lix. 21; Exod. xxix. 43–45.—[c]Gen. xv. 6; Heb. iv. 2, 6; Exod. xii. 27, 28; 2 Cor. vi. 16–18, vii. 1.—[d]Ps. lxxxiv. 1, 28, 4, 10, lxv. 4, xxxvi. 7, 8.—[e]Ps. xxiii. 6, xxvii. 4; Rev. ii. 3, 10; Gal. vi. 9; Heb. x. 23–25, xii. 3.

EXPLICATION. — This is the first thing that God requireth us to attend unto in the celebration of the ordinances of his worship, — namely, that we therein *sanctify his name*, the greatest duty that we are called unto in this world. This he lays down as the general rule of all we do herein: Lev. x. 3, "I will," saith he, "be sanctified in them that come nigh me, and before all the people I will be glorified." Whatever we do in his worship, we must do it that he may be sanctified, or whatever we do is an abomination to him. Now, the principal ways how we may herein sanctify the name of God are expressed; as, —

First, When in every ordinance we consider his appointment of it, and submit our souls and consciences unto his *authority* therein; which if we observe any thing in his worship but what he hath appointed we cannot do. Not formality, not custom, not the precepts of men, not any thing but the *authority* and command of God, is to be respected in this obedience. This is the first thing that faith regards in divine worship; it rests not in any thing, closeth not with any thing, but what it discerns that God hath commanded, and therein it eyes his authority as he requireth it: Mal. i. 6, "If I be a father, where is mine honour? and if I be a master, where is my fear?" Rom. xiv. 11, "As I live, saith the Lord, every knee shall bow to me, and every tongue shall confess to God." Reverence, then, unto the authority of God appointing his worship is a principal means of sanctifying the name of God therein. This was the solemn sanction of all his institutions of old: Deut. vi. 4–7, "Hear, O Israel: The LORD our God is one LORD: and thou shalt love the LORD thy God with all thine heart, and with all thy soul, and with all thy might. And these words, which I command thee this day, shall be in thy heart: and thou shalt teach them diligently unto thy children." And the observation of them he presseth on this account, that the people might fear that "glorious and fearful name, THE LORD THY GOD," Deut. xxviii. 58; which name he had so often engaged in his commands, saying, "Thou shalt do it; I am the LORD." And in the New Testament, our Lord Jesus Christ proposeth his authority as the foundation of his commanding, and our observation of all the institutions of the gospel: Matt. xxviii. 18–20, "Jesus came and spake unto them, saying, All power is given unto me in heaven and in earth. Go ye therefore, and teach all nations, baptizing them in the name of the Father, and of the Son, and of the Holy Ghost: teaching them to observe all things whatsoever I have commanded you." And he is to be considered in all our obedience as the great and only lawgiver of his church; as the "one lawgiver, who is able to save and destroy," James iv. 12; the sovereign Lord over his "house," Heb. iii. 4–6, unto whom every knee is to bow and every conscience to be in subjection: and he who heareth not his voice is to be cut off from the people of God: Acts iii. 23, "It shall come to pass, that every soul, which will not hear that prophet, shall be destroyed from among the people."

Secondly, God hath frequently promised his *special presence* in and with his instituted ordinances of old, both unto the *things* themselves and the *places* wherein they were according to his appointment to be celebrated, those places being also his special institution. Under the New Testament, all difference of and respect unto place is taken away: John iv. 21, 23, "The hour cometh when ye shall neither in this mountain, nor yet at Jerusalem, worship the Father. But the hour cometh, and now is, when the true worshippers shall worship the Father in spirit and truth: for the Father seeketh such to worship him." And we are commanded in *all places* equally to make our prayers and supplications. But his presence is promised and continued with the due celebration of the things themselves by him appointed for his service: Matt. xxviii. 20, "Teaching them to observe all things whatsoever I have commanded you: and, lo, I am with you alway, even unto the end of the world." In them is the "tabernacle of God with men," and he "dwells among them, and they are his people," Rev. xxi. 3; the promise of Christ being, that "where two or three are gathered together in his name, there he will be in the midst of them," Matt. xviii. 19, 20. And this promised presence of God, or Christ, consisteth, — 1. In the power and efficacy which he by his Spirit implants upon his ordinances to communicate his grace and mercy unto his church, it being his covenant that his Spirit shall accompany his word for ever unto that purpose, Isa. lix. 21. 2. In the special blessing which he gives his people in those duties, both in the acceptance of them and testifying his good-will unto them: Exod. xxix. 42, 43, 45, "At the door of the tabernacle of the congregation, there I will meet with the children of Israel, and the tabernacle shall be sanctified by my glory. And I will dwell among the children of Israel, and will be their God;" Zech. ii. 10, 11; Ezek. xx. 40, 41, "I will accept you with your sweet savour;" chap. xliii. 27; — in both giving them intimate communion with himself by Jesus Christ, 1 John i. 3. By all these he gives that special presence, which he requires an especial reverence and regard of faith unto, whereby his name is yet farther sanctified.

Thirdly, God hath given *special promises*, or *promises of his special grace*, unto them that attend upon him in his worship in a due manner. And hereunto also belongs that sacred relation which, by virtue of divine institution, is between the sacramental elements and the especial graces of the covenant which they exhibit and confirm; and the mixing of these promises with faith, according as they are appropriated unto any particular institution, belongs also to the right sanctification of the mind of God. So also, —

Fourthly, Doth our *delight* in them. Now, this delight in the worship of God, so much commended in the Scripture, and proposed unto our example, consists not in any carnal self-pleasing, or satisfaction in the outward modes or manner of the performance of divine worship; but it is a holy, soul-refreshing contemplation on the will, wisdom, grace, and condescension of God, in that he is pleased, of his own sovereign mere will and grace, so to manifest himself unto such poor sinful creatures as we are, so to condescend unto our weakness, so to communicate himself unto us, so to excite and draw forth our souls unto himself, and to give us such pledges of his gracious intercourse with us by Jesus Christ. By the contemplation of these things is the soul drawn forth to delight in God.

Lastly, Whereas great *opposition* lies oftentimes against the church's obedience unto God in this matter, and much persecution befalls it on that account, — great weariness also being apt, from the remainders of unbelief, carnal wisdom, indwelling sin, weakness of the flesh in believers themselves, to arise in the course thereof, and many temptations also beset them on every hand, to turn them aside from the way of truth and holiness, — constancy and perseverance in the due and orderly celebration of all the ordinances of the gospel belongs unto this duty. And this *perseverance* respecteth both the things themselves and the manner of their performance, both which are of the highest concernment for us diligently to attend unto.

1. As to the *things themselves*. Herein do we principally glorify God and give due honour unto

Jesus Christ, when we abide in our professed subjection unto him and observance of his commands against difficulties, oppositions, and persecutions. This he taketh notice of, Rev. ii. 13, "Thou holdest fast my name, and hast not denied my faith, even in those days wherein Antipas was my faithful martyr, who was slain among you, where Satan dwelleth." And this he requireth of us indispensably if we will be his disciples, or ever hope to obtain the reward: Matt. x. 38, 39, "He that taketh not his cross, and followeth after me, is not worthy of me;" and it is "he that shall endure unto the end" that shall be "saved," chap. xxiv. 13. And unto them who are "faithful unto death," and them alone, doth he give the "crown of life," Rev. ii. 10; giving us caution not to "lose those things which we have wrought," that we may "receive a full reward," 2 John 8.

2. And as to the manner of their performance, two things are to be regarded in this duty of perseverance, and the sanctification of the name of God therein:— (1.) The *inward principle* of our obedience, our faith and love; which are to be preserved from decay: Rev. ii. 4, 5, "I have somewhat against thee, because thou hast left thy first love. Remember therefore from whence thou art fallen, and repent, and do the first works." Chap. iii. 3, "Remember how thou hast received and heard, and hold fast, and repent." (2.) The *outward manner* of observance; which is to be kept entire, according to the primitive institution of Christ: 1 Cor. xi. 23, "I have received of the Lord that which also I delivered unto you," — not admitting of any corruptions in it, to avoid the greatest trouble: Gal. v. 11, "And I, brethren, if I yet preach circumcision, why do I yet suffer persecution?"

Q. 9 *How do we in our observation profess our subjection unto the Lord Jesus Christ and his gospel?*

A. In that being all of them, first *appointed* by him as the head, lawgiver, and king of his church; and, secondly, made by him the *ensigns* and tokens of his kingdom and subjects; in their due observation principally consists that *profession* of him and his name which he so often calleth us unto, and so indispensably requireth at our hands.—Matt. xxviii. 18–20; 1 Cor. xi. 23; Heb. iii. 6, xii. 25; John xiii. 13, viii. 31, xiv. 15, 21, 23, xv. 14, 17, xiii. 35, xv. 14; Luke ix. 26; Rom. x. 10; 1 John ii. 3, 4.

EXPLICATION. — The ground and reason of this duty is evident. The Lord Jesus Christ straitly enjoins all his disciples the *profession* of his name, and lays it on them as indispensable unto salvation: Rom. x. 10, "With the heart man believeth unto righteousness, and with the mouth confession," or profession, "is made unto salvation;" John xii. 42–45. Now, this profession of the name of Christ, which is so much abused and mistaken in the world, consists in the keeping of his commandments: John xv. 14, "Ye are my friends, if ye do whatsoever I command you." So also, Matt. xxviii. 20, his disciples are to be taught to do and observe whatever he commandeth. Now, whereas he is the head and king of the church, the next immediate and special lawgiver of it, appointing unto it all his ordinances and its whole worship, as it becomes him who is lord of the house, the institutions of the gospel worship are his most especial commands; and in their observation consists that *profession* of him which he requires of us; therein doth he call them out of the world by profession whom he hath redeemed out of it by his blood, 2 Cor. vi. 15–18; Rev. v. 9. In these he exerciseth his kingly or lordly power over his church, Heb. iii. 6; and in the willing obedience of his people, gathering themselves unto the ensigns of his rule, he is glorified in the world.

Q. 10 *How do we in and by them build up ourselves in our most holy faith?*

A. By the exercise of that communion with God in Christ Jesus which, in their due observation, he graciously invites and admits us unto, for the increase of his grace in us, and the testification of his love and good-will towards us.—Gen. xvii. 10; Lev. xxvi. 11, 12; Prov. ix. 5, 6; Ezek. xxxvi. 27, 28; Zech. xiv. 16, 17; Matt. xxvi. 27, 28; Rom. vi. 3.

EXPLICATION. — The next and principal ends of all instituted worship, in respect of believers, are, the increase of the grace of God in them, their edification in their most holy faith, and the testification of the good-will of God unto them: Eph. iv. 11–16, "And he gave some, apostles; and some, prophets; and some, evangelists; and some, pastors and teachers; for the perfecting of the saints, for the work of the ministry, for the edifying of the body of Christ: till we all come in the unity of the faith, and of the knowledge of the Son of God, unto a perfect man, unto the measure of the stature of the fulness of Christ: that we henceforth be no more children, tossed to and fro, and carried about with every wind of doctrine, by the sleight of men, and cunning craftiness, whereby they lie in wait to deceive; but speaking the truth in love, may grow up into him in all things, which is the head, even Christ: from whom the whole body fitly joined together and compacted by that which every joint supplieth, according to the effectual working in the measure of every part, maketh increase of the body unto the edifying of itself in love." Whence, also, is that prayer of the apostle for the blessing of God upon the church, in the use of them: Eph. iii. 16–19, "That he would grant you, according to the riches of his glory, to be strengthened with might by his Spirit in the inner man; that Christ may dwell in your hearts by faith; that ye, being rooted and grounded in love, may be able to comprehend with all saints what is the breadth, and length, and depth, and height; and to know the love of Christ, which passeth knowledge, that ye might be filled with all the fulness of God." For these ends, and with a design to have them accomplished in and upon their souls, ought they to attend unto them: James i. 21, "Receive with meekness the engrafted word, which is able to save your souls." 1 Pet. ii. 2, "As new-born babes, desire the sincere milk of the word, that ye may grow thereby." Unto the effecting of these ends, especially the increase and establishment of our faith, are they suited and appointed of God; whereon all their efficacy doth depend. In their due observation doth God give out that supply of grace which he hath promised, Eph. iii. 16–19. And thus also is faith exercised in an especial manner; which is the only ordinary means of its growth and increase. Habits, both *acquired* and *infused*, are increased and strengthened by frequent acts on suitable objects: Hos. vi. 3, "Then shall we know, if we follow on to know the Lord." In the celebration of gospel ordinances, God in Christ proposeth himself in an intimate manner to the believing soul as his God and reward; and his love in Christ, in an especial manner, in some ordinances. So doth Christ also exhibit himself thereunto: Rev. iii. 20, "Behold, I stand at the door and knock: if any man hear my voice, and open the door, I will come in to him, and will sup with him, and he with me." Faith, therefore, directed by the word to rest in God, to receive the Lord Christ in the observation of his ordinances, is excited, increased, strengthened, and that in answer unto the appointment and promises of God.

Q. 11 *How are mutual love and communion among believers testified and confirmed in their observation?*

A. In that they are appointed by the Lord Christ for that end, and in their own nature, as attended unto in their assemblies, are in an especial manner suited unto that purpose.—John xiii. 35; 1 Cor. x. 16, 17, xi. 18, 19; Eph. iv. 3–6.

EXPLICATION. — The principles of mutual, spiritual love among believers arise from their relation unto *one Father*: Matt. xxiii. 9, "One is your Father, which is in heaven," who giveth unto all them that believe in Christ "power to become the sons of God," John i. 12; and their being all children of the same family, — that family in heaven and earth which is called after the name of God, the Father of it, as the Father of our Lord Jesus Christ, Eph. iii. 14, 15; — and unto Christ Jesus as their elder brother, who "is not ashamed to call them brethren," Heb. ii. 11, being by him born of God; — and from their participation of one and the self-same Spirit, which dwelleth in them, as they are "the temple of God, and the Spirit of God dwelleth in them," 1 Cor. iii. 16; as also in all the fruits of that one Spirit, 1 Cor. xii. 4–8, and in that *one faith* and hope whereunto they are called: Eph. iv. 3–6, "Endeavouring to keep the unity of the Spirit in the bond of peace. There is one body, and one Spirit, even as ye are called in one hope of your calling; one Lord, one faith, one baptism, one God and Father of all, who is above all, and through all, and in you all." And that love which is not built on these principles and foundations is not evangelical, whatever other ground it may have, or occasion it may pretend unto. Communion of saints consists in their mutual love, duly exercised according to rule; and all communion is an effect of union. In union therefore must lie the springs of love, and this consists in a joint incorporation of believers into Christ; "for as the body is one, and hath many members, and all the members of that one body being many, are one body, so also is Christ; for by one Spirit we are all baptized into one body;" — and this they have by the means before mentioned, namely, their adoption, faith, and inhabitation of the Spirit. Now, in the joint celebration of the ordinances of God's worship, they all together make profession of these principles, and act that one faith, hope, and love jointly, whereof they are made partakers, and thereby grow up more and more into the head "by that which every joint supplieth," Eph. iv. 16. And some of them are peculiarly designed by the Lord Christ for the testification of their love and union among themselves: 1 Cor. x. 16, 17, "The cup of blessing which we bless, is it not the communion of the blood of Christ? The bread which we break, is it not the communion of the body of Christ? For we being many are one bread, and one body: for we are all partakers of that one bread."

Q. 12 *What is principally to be attended unto by us in the manner of the celebration of the worship of God, and observation of the institutions and ordinances of the gospel?*

A. That we observe and do all whatsoever the

Lord Christ hath commanded us to observe, in the way that he hath prescribed; and that we add nothing unto or in the observation of them that is of man's invention or appointment.—Deut. iv. 2, xii. 32; Jer. vii. 27; Matt. xv. 9, 13, xvii. 5; Col. ii. 6; Matt. xxviii. 20 Heb. iii. 3–6; 1 Cor. xi. 23; Rev. xxii. 18, 19; 1 Chron. xvi. 7; Isa. xxix. 13.

EXPLICATION. — This was in part spoken to before on the third question, where it was showed that the Scripture is the only way and means whereby God hath revealed what that worship is which he will accept in and of the church. Here, moreover, as to the duty of the church in this matter, three things are asserted:—

First, That we are to observe and *do all whatsoever* the Lord Christ hath commanded us to observe. This lies plain in the command, Mat. xxviii. 20, "Teaching them to observe all things whatsoever I have commanded you." And we are directed unto it in the injunction given us from heaven, to "hear," — that is, to obey him in all things, Matt. xvii. 5, he being the prophet to whose teachings and instructions we owe obedience, on pain of extermination from among the people of God, 1 Cor. x. 16, 17, xi. 18, 19; Acts iii. 22, 23. Whatever he hath appointed, commanded, revealed as the will of God to be observed in or about the worship of God, that is to kept and observed by the church inviolably; for if we are his friends and disciples, we will keep his commandments. No disuse, of what continuance soever, can discharge us from the observation of institutions. After the feast of tabernacles had been disused from the times of Joshua unto the return from the captivity, the restoration of it was required of God and accepted with him, Neh. viii. 17. No abuse, of how high a nature soever, can absolve us from obedience unto an institution, 1 Cor. xi. 20–23. After the great abuse of the Lord's supper in that church, the apostle recalls them again unto the observation of it, according to the institution of Christ. And after the defilement of all the ordinances of the gospel, under the antichristian apostasy, yet the temple and the alter are to be measured again, Rev. xi. 1, and the tabernacle of God was again to be raised amongst men, chap. xxi. 3. No opposition, no persecution, can give the church a dispensation wholly to omit and lay aside the use of any thing that the Lord Christ hath commanded to be observed in the worship of God, whilst we are under the obligation of that great rule, Acts iv. 19, "Whether it be right in the sight of God to hearken unto you more than unto God, judge ye." It is true, in the observation of positive institutions, we may have regard unto rules and prescriptions of prudence, as to times, places, and seasons, that by no inadvertency or miscarriage of ours, or advantage taken by the adversaries of the truth, the edification of the church be hindered; — so the disciples met with "the doors shut for fear of the Jews," John xx. 19; and Paul met with the disciples in the night, in "an upper chamber," for the celebration of all the ordinances of the church, Acts xx. 7, 8; — yet, as to the obligation unto their observation, it indispensably binds us, and that always, and that as to all the institutions of Christ whatever: Heb. x. 25, "Not forsaking the assembling of ourselves together, as the manner of some is; but exhorting one another: and so much the more, as ye see the day approaching." To dispense with Christ's commands practically is unlawful, much more doctrinally, most of all *authoritatively*, as the pope takes on himself to do. This, then, is the church's duty, to search out all the commands of Christ recorded in the gospel, and to yield obedience unto them. We are not, in this matter, to take up merely with what we find in practice amongst others, no, though they be men good or holy. The duty of the church, and, consequently, of every member of it in his place and station, is to search the Scriptures, to inquire into the mind of Christ, and that with hearts and minds prepared unto a due observation of whatever shall be discovered to be his will.

Secondly, Whatever belongs unto the worship of God, in the *way or manner* whereby any of the ordinances of Christ is to be performed, comes also under the command of Christ, which is duly to be attended unto and observed. Indeed, whatever is of this nature appointed by Christ, it doth therefore belong to the worship of God; and what is not so appointed neither doth nor can be any part thereof. Of this nature is the celebration of all other ordinances with prayer, for every thing is "sanctified by the word of God and prayer," 1 Tim. iv. 5; of some of them indispensably in the assemblies of the church, 1 Cor. x. 16, 17, xi. 20, 24, 25, 33; with care in the observation of the general rules of love, modesty, condescension, and prudence, "doing all things decently and in order," 1 Cor. xi. 33, xiv. 40; gestures in some sacred actions, Matt. xxvi. 20, 26–28; John xiii. 23; — all which the church is diligently to inquire into, as things that belong to the pattern of the house of God, "the goings out thereof and the comings in thereof, the forms thereof and the ordinances thereof, with the laws thereof," promised to be showed unto it, Ezek. xliii. 11. To attend carefully to their observation is its duty, being left at liberty as to all other circumstances;

which no authority of man can give any real relation to the worship of God unto. Therein lies the exercise of that spirit of wisdom and revelation in the knowledge of the mystery of the gospel, which is given unto the church, Eph. i. 17, 18. It was the wisdom of the ancient church to do and observe all that God appointed, in the way and manner that he had prescribed for their observance: Deut. iv. 5, 6, "Behold, I have taught you statutes and judgments, even as the LORD my God commanded me. Keep therefore and do them; for this is your wisdom and your understanding." And herein is the command of Christ kept inviolate and unblamable. The persuasion of some, that the Lord hath not prescribed all things wherein his worship is concerned, seems to proceed from a negligence in inquiring after what he hath so prescribed. And when once that persuasion is entertained, all farther inquiry is superseded and despised; for to what end should any one seek after that which he is satisfied cannot be found? as that which is not cannot be. But this mistake will be elsewhere more fully discovered.

Thirdly, A principal part of the duty of the church in this matter is, to take care that nothing be admitted or practised in the worship of God, or as belonging thereunto, which is not instituted and appointed by the Lord Christ. In its care, faithfulness, and watchfulness herein consists the principal part of its loyalty unto the Lord Jesus, as the head, king, and lawgiver of his church; and which to stir us up into, he hath left so many severe interdictions and prohibitions in his word against all *additions* to his commands, upon any pretence whatever; of which afterward.

Q. 13 *Are not some institutions of the New Testament ceased as to any obligation unto their observation, and therefore now rightly disused?*

A. ᵃSome symbolical tokens of moral duties, occasionally used, only for present instruction in those duties, are mentioned in the gospel, without any intention to oblige believers unto the formal constant use and repetition of them; and ᵇsome temporary appointments relating unto gifts in the church, bestowed only for a season on the first plantation of the gospel, are ceased; — but ᶜno institution or command of Christ, given unto the whole church, relating unto the evangelical administration of the new covenant, for the use and benefit of all believers, doth or shall cease to the end of the world, nor can be wholly omitted without a violation of the authority of Jesus Christ himself. —ᵃJohn xiii. 12–15; Rom. xvi. 16; 1 Cor. xvi. 20; 1 Tim. v. 10. —ᵇMark vi. 13; James v. 14. —ᶜMatt. xxviii. 20; 1 Tim. vi. 14; 1 Cor. xi. 26.

EXPLICATION. — Mention is made in the Scriptures of sundry things practised by the Lord Christ and his apostles, which being then in common use among men, were occasionally made by them symbolical instructions in moral duties. Such were washing of feet by one another, the holy kiss, and the like. But there being no more in them but a sanctified use directed unto the present civil customs and usages, the commands given concerning them respect not the outward action, nor appointed any continuance of them, being peculiarly suited unto the state of things and persons in those countries; as, John xiii. 12–15, "After he had washed their feet, and had taken his garments, and was set down again, he said unto them, Know ye what I have done to you? Ye call me Master and

Lord: and ye say well; for so I am. If I then, your Lord and Master, have washed your feet; ye also ought to wash one another's feet. For I have given you an example, that ye should do as I have done to you." It is evident in the moral duty of brotherly love, in condescension and mutual helpfulness, to be expressed in all necessary offices as occasion doth require, that is the thing which Jesus Christ here enjoined his disciples, and leads them to by his own example in an office of love then in use in those parts. The same is to be said of the "holy kiss," Rom. xvi. 16; which was a temporary, occasional token of entire love, which may, in answer thereunto, be expressed by any sober usage of salutation amongst men to the same purpose. But the things themselves were not instituted for any continuance, nor do represent any special grace of the new covenant, which is inseparable from every institution of gospel worship properly so called. Common usages or practices, therefore, directed to be used in a due manner and unto a proper end, where they are used, make them not institutions of worship. Neither have they in them, as so commanded or directed, any one thing that concurs to the constitution of a gospel ordinance; for neither had they their rise in the authority of Christ, nor is any continuance of them enjoined, nor any promise annexed unto them, nor any grace of the new covenant represented or exhibited in them.

Besides, there were in the first churches, continued for a while, certain *extraordinary gifts*, that had their effects visible on the outward senses of men, and tended not immediately unto the edification of the churches in their faith, but unto the conviction of others, and vindication of the authority of them by whom the gospel was preached and propagated. Such was that *gift of healing* the sick: which being an especial effect of the Holy Ghost for the advantage of the church in those days, in some places it was accompanied by anointing with oil; but this being no universal practice, and used only in the exercise of a gift extraordinary, whose use and being has long since ceased, it never was appointed nor intended to be of continuance in the church, which is not tied by the Lord Christ to the empty signs and shadows of things whose substance is not enjoyed. Besides, no spiritual grace of the covenant was ever intimated, sealed, or exhibited by that usage of anointing with oil. The first mention of it is, Mark vi. 13, where its practice is reckoned among the effects of that extraordinary power which the Lord Christ committed unto his twelve disciples on their first sending out, and is referred unto the same series of miracles which they wrought in pursuit and by virtue thereof: "They cast out many devils, and anointed with oil many that were sick, and healed them." And by what is there recorded, the subsequent mention of it, James v. 14, is to be regulated. But now, unto a real evangelical institution of worship, it is required, — 1. That it be a command of Christ, manifested by his word or example proposed unto our imitation, Matt. xxviii. 20; 2. That it be given and enjoined unto the whole church, with the limitation of its administration expressed in the word, 1 Cor. xi. 25; 3. That, unto the due performance of it, gospel grace be required in them that attend unto it; 4. That it teach, or represent, or seal, or improve some grace of the covenant, and have a promise of acceptation annexed unto it. And whatever is thus appointed, the church is indispensably to continue in the observation of, unto the end of the world.

Q. 14 *May not the church find out, and appoint to be observed, such religious rites as, being adjoined unto the celebration of God's instituted worship, may further the devotion of the worshippers, and render the worship itself in its performance more decent, beautiful, and orderly, as the appointing of images, and the like?*

A. All acceptable devotion in them that worship God is the effect of faith, which respects the precepts and promises of God alone. And the comeliness and beauty of gospel worship consisteth in its relation unto God by Jesus Christ, as the merciful high priest over his house, with the glorious administration of the Spirit therein. The order also of it lieth in the due and regular observation of all that Christ hath appointed. And therefore all such inventions are in themselves needless and useless, and, because forbidden, unlawful to be observed.—Rom. i. 21, xiv. 23; Heb. iv. 2, xi. 4, 6; Deut. xiii. 4, xxvii. 10, xxx. 2, 8, 20, xi. 27; Matt. xvii. 5; Isa. xxix. 13; Eph. ii. 18; 2 Cor. iii. 7–11; Heb. x. 19–22; John iv. 21–23; 1 Cor. xiv. 25; Matt. xxviii. 20; Exod. xx. 4; Deut. iv. 2; Matt. xv. 13; Deut. xii. 32, xvii. 3.

EXPLICATION. — Three things are usually pleaded in the justification of the observance of such *rites* and ceremonies in the worship of God:— First, That they tend unto the furtherance of the *devotion* of the worshippers; secondly, That they render the worship itself *comely* and beautiful; thirdly, That they are the great preservers of *order* in the celebration thereof. And therefore on these accounts they may be instituted or appointed by some, and observed by all.

But things are indeed quite otherwise: "God is a Spirit, and will be worshipped in spirit and in truth," John iv. 24. And no devotion is acceptable unto him, but what proceedeth from and is an effect of faith; for "without faith it is impossible to please God," Heb. xi. 6. And faith in all things respects the commands and authority of God; for saith he, "In vain do they worship me, who teach for doctrines the commandments of men," Matt. xv. 9; and he rejecteth all that honour which is given him by those whose fear towards him or worship of him is "taught by the precepts of men," Isa. xxix. 13. These things, therefore, being utterly destitute of divine authority, they can no way further or promote the devotion of the worshippers. What natural or carnal affections may be excited by them, — as men may "inflame themselves with idols," Isa. lvii. 5, — or what outward, outside devotion they may direct unto or excite, is uncertain; but that they are no means of stirring up the grace of God in the hearts of believers, or of the increase or strengthening of their faith, — which things alone God accepts in gospel worship, — seeing they are not appointed by him for any such purpose, is most certain: for to say that any thing will effectually stir up devotion, — that is, excite, strengthen, or increase grace in the heart towards God, — that is not of his own appointment, is on the one hand to reflect on his wisdom and care towards his church, as if he had been wanting towards it in things so necessary, which he declares against, Isa. v. 4, "What," saith he, "could have been done more to my vineyard, that I have not done in it?" so on the other, it extols the wisdom of men above what is meet to ascribe unto it. Shall men find out that which God would not, or could not, in matters of so great importance unto his glory and the souls that obey him? Yea, and it cannot be but that attendance unto them and their effects must needs divert the mind from those proper spiritual actings of faith and grace which is its duty to attend unto. And this is evidently seen in them who, indulging to themselves in their observation in multiplied instances, as in the church of Rome, have changed the whole spiritual worship of the church into a theatrical, pompous show of carnal devotion.

Secondly, The *comeliness* and beauty of gospel worship doth not in the least depend upon them nor their observation. The apostle doth in sundry places expressly compare the spiritual worship of the gospel with that of the law, whilst the church had a *worldly sanctuary* and carnal ordinances, Heb. ix. 1. And although it be most evident that the worship of the Old Testament did, for the glory and ornaments of outward ceremonies, and the splendour of their observation, far exceed and excel that worship which God commands now, as suitable unto the simplicity of the gospel, yet doth the apostle prefer this, for glory, comeliness, and beauty, unspeakably above the other; which manifests that these things can have no respect unto outward rites and ceremonies, wherein the chief admirers of them can no way vie for glory with the old worship of the temple. So the apostle, 2 Cor. iii. 7–11, "If the ministration of death, written and engraven in stones, was glorious, so that the children of Israel could not steadfastly behold the face of Moses for the glory of his countenance; which glory was to be done away: how shall not the ministration of the spirit be rather glorious? For if the ministration of condemnation be glory, much more doth the ministration of righteousness exceed in glory. For even that which was made glorious had no glory in this respect, by reason of the glory that excelleth. For if that which is done away was glorious, much more that which remaineth is glorious." He compareth the two ministrations and the several worships of the law and gospel, preferring this unspeakably above the other, sufficiently manifesting that the glory of it consisteth not in any pompous observance of outward ceremonies. And elsewhere he declareth that indeed it doth consist in its relation to God in Christ, with the liberty and boldness of the worshippers to enter into the holy place, unto the throne of grace, under the ministry of their merciful and faithful high priest, being enabled thereunto by the Spirit of adoption and supplications; for therein, "through Christ, we have access by one Spirit unto the Father," Eph. ii. 18; as it is expressed, Heb. x. 19–21, "Having therefore boldness to enter into the holiest by the blood of Jesus, by a new and living way, which he hath consecrated for us, through the vail, that is to say, his flesh; and having an high priest over the house of God; let us draw near with a true heart in full assurance of faith, having our hearts sprinkled from an evil conscience, and our bodies washed with pure water." This is the glory of gospel worship and the beauty of it; whose consideration whilst the minds of men are diverted from, to look for beauty in the outward preparation of ceremonies, they lose the privilege purchased for believers by the blood of Christ. Instead, then, of furthering the beauty and comeliness of gospel worship, they are apt to lead men into a dangerous error and mistake, — as, upon a due consideration, will appear to be mean and carnal, and far beneath those ceremonies and ordinances of the Old Testament, which yet, in comparison of the worship of the gospel, are called "worldly, carnal, beggarly," and are said to have "no glory."

Thirdly, They do not in the least tend unto the preservation of due *order* in the celebration of divine worship. All *order* consists in the due observation of *rule*. The rules of actions are either natural or of his special appointment. Both these take place in religious worship; the institutions or commands of Christ containing the substance thereof, in their observation principally consists the order of it. Whatever is of circumstance in the manner of its performance, not capable of especial determination, as emerging or arising only *occasionally*, upon the doing of that which is appointed at this or that time, in this or that place, and the like, is left unto the rule of *moral prudence*, in whose observation their order doth consist. But the superaddition of ceremonies necessarily belonging neither to the institutions of worship nor unto those circumstances whose disposal falls under the rule of moral prudence, neither doth nor can add any thing unto the due order of gospel worship; so that they are altogether needless and useless in the worship of God. Neither is this the whole of the inconvenience wherewith their observance is attended; for although they are not in particular and expressly in the Scripture forbidden, — for it was simply impossible that all instances wherein the wit of man might exercise its invention in such things should be reckoned up and condemned, — yet they fall directly under those severe prohibitions which God hath recorded to secure his worship from all such *additions* unto it, of what sort soever. Yea, the main design of the second precept is to forbid all making unto ourselves any such things in the worship of God, to add unto what he hath appointed; whereof an instance is given in that of *making and worshipping images*, the most common way that the sons of men were then prone to transgress by against the institutions of God. And this sense and understanding of the commandment is secured by those ensuing prohibitions against the adding any thing at all unto the commands of God in his worship: Deut. iv. 2, "Ye shall not add unto the word which I command you, neither shall ye diminish ought from it, that ye may keep the commandments of the Lord your God." Deut. xii. 32, "What thing soever I command you, observe to do it: thou shalt not add thereto, nor diminish from it;" chap. xvii. 3. To the same purpose were the places before mentioned, Matt. xv. 9, etc.; as also that severe rule applied by our Saviour unto the additions of the Pharisees, verse 13, "Every plant, which my heavenly Father hath not planted, shall be rooted up."

And there is yet farther evidence contributed unto this intention of the command, from those places where such evils and corruptions as were particularly forbidden in the worship of God are condemned, not on the special account of their being so forbidden, but on that more general, of being introduced without warrant from God's institutions or commands: Jer. vii. 31, "They have built the high places of Tophet, which is in the valley of the son of Hinnom, to burn their sons and daughters in the fire; which I commanded not, neither came it into my heart." Chap. xix. 5, "They have built also the high places of Baal, to burn their sons with fire for burnt offerings unto Baal, which I commanded not, nor spake it, neither came it into my mind." These things were particularly forbidden; but yet God here condemns them as coming under the general evil of making additions unto his commands, — doing that which he commanded not, nor did it ever enter into his heart.

The Papists say, indeed, that all *additions corrupting* the worship of God are forbidden, but such as further, adorn, and preserve it are not so; which implies a contradiction, for whereas every *addition* is principally a *corruption* because it is an addition, under which notion it is forbidden (and that in the worship of God which is forbidden is a corruption of it), there can be no such preserving, adorning addition, unless we allow a preserving and adorning corruption. Neither is it of more force which is pleaded by them, that the additions which they make belong not unto the *substance* of the worship of God, but unto the *circumstances* of it; for every circumstance observed religiously, or to be observed in the worship of God, is of the substance of it, as were all those ceremonious observances of the law, which had the same respect in the prohibitions of adding with the most weighty things whatsoever.

Q. 15 *Whence may it appear that the right and due observation of instituted worship is of great importance unto the glory of God, and of high concernment unto the souls of men?*

A. This is fully taught in the Scriptures; as, [a]God would never accept in any state of the church, before or since the fall, moral obedience without the observation of some institutions as trials, tokens, and pledges of that obedience. And [b]in their use and signification by his appointment they nearly concern the principal mysteries of his will and grace; and [c]by their celebration is he glorified in the world. And, therefore, [d]as he hath made blessed promises to his people, to grant them his presence and to bless them in their use; so, ᵉbeing the tokens of the marriage relation that is between him and them, with respect unto them alone he calls himself "a jealous God," and ᶠhath actually exercised signal severity towards the neglecters, corrupters, or abusers of them.—ᵃGen. ii. 16, 17, iv. 3–5, xvii. 9–11; Exod. xii. 21, xx.; Matt. xxviii. 19, 20,xxvi. 26, 27; Eph. iv. 11, 12; Rev. i. 13, xxi. 3.—ᵇGen. xvii. 10; Exod. xii. 23, 24; Rom. vi. 3–5; Matt. xxvi. 26–28; 1 Cor. xi. 23–26.—ᶜSee questions the eighth and ninth.—ᵈExod. xxix. 42, 43, 45; Deut. xiv. 23, 24; Ps. cxxxiii. 3; Matt. xviii. 20; Rev. xxi. 3.—ᵉExod xx. 5; Deut. iv. 23, 24; Josh. xxiv. 19; Ezek. xvi.—ᶠLev. x. 1, 2; Num. xvi. 1–40; 1 Sam. ii. 27–34; 2 Sam. vi. 6, 7; 2 Chron. xxvi. 16–21; 1 Cor. xi. 30.

EXPLICATION. — For the most part, the instituted worship of God is neglected and despised in the world. Some are utterly regardless of it, supposing that if they attend, after their manner, unto moral obedience, that neither God nor themselves are much concerned in this matter of his worship. Others think the disposal and ordering of it to be so left unto men, that, as to the manner of its performance, they may do with it as it seems right in their own eyes; and some follow them therein, as willingly walking after their commandments, without any respect unto the will or authority of God. But the whole Scripture gives us utterly another account of this matter. The *honour* of God in this world, the *trial* of our faith and obedience, the *order* and beauty of the church, the *exaltation* of Christ in our professed subjection to him, and the *saving* of our souls in the ways of his appointment, are therein laid upon the due and right observance of instituted worship; and they who are negligent about these things, whatever they pretend, have no real respect unto anything that is called religion. First, therefore, in every state and condition of the church, God hath given his ordinances of worship as the touchstone and trial of its faith and obedience; so that they by whom they are neglected do openly refuse to come unto God's trial. In the state of innocency, the trial of Adam's obedience, according to the law of nature, was in and by the institution of the *tree of life, and of the knowledge of good and evil*: Gen ii. 16, 17, "And the LORD God commanded the man, saying, Of every tree of the garden thou mayest freely eat: but of the tree of the knowledge of good and evil, thou shalt not eat of it: for in the day that thou eatest thereof thou shalt surely die." This was the first institution of God, and it was given unto the church in the state of innocency and purity. And in our first parents' neglect of attending thereunto did they transgress the whole law of their creation, as failing in their duty in that which was appointed for their trial in the whole: Chap. iii. 11, "Hast thou eaten of the tree, whereof I commanded thee that thou shouldest not eat?", etc. And the church in his family after the fall, built upon the promise, was tried also in the matter of instituted worship. Nor was there any discovery of the wickedness of Cain, or approbation of the faith of Abel, until they came to be proved in their *sacrifices*; a new part of God's instituted worship, the first in the state and condition of sin and the fall whereinto it was brought: Gen. iv. 3–5, "In process of time it came to pass, that Cain brought of the fruit of the ground an offering unto the LORD. And Abel, he also brought of the firstlings of his flock and of the fat thereof. And the LORD had respect unto Abel and to his offering: but unto Cain and his offering he had not respect."

The ground whereof the apostle declares, Heb. xi. 4, "By faith Abel offered unto God a more excellent sacrifice than Cain, by which he obtained witness that he was righteous, God testifying of his gifts." In the observation of that first institution, given to the church in the state of the fall, did Abel receive a testimony of his being justified and accepted with God. Afterward, when Abraham was called, and peculiarly separated to bear forth the name of God in the world, and to become the spring of the church for future ages, he had the institution of *circumcision* given him for the trial of his obedience; the law and condition whereof was, that he who observed it not should be esteemed an alien from the covenant of God, and be cut off from his people: Gen. xvii. 9–11, "God said unto Abraham, Thou shalt keep my covenant, thou, and thy seed after thee in their generations. This is my covenant, which ye shall keep, between me and you and thy seed after thee; Every man-child among you shall be circumcised." Verse 14, "And the uncircumcised man-child whose flesh of his foreskin is not circumcised, that soul shall be cut off from his people; he hath broken my covenant." And in like manner, so soon as ever his posterity were to be collected into a new church state and order, God gave the ordinance of the *passover*: Exod. xii. 24, "Ye shall observe this thing for an ordinance to thee and to thy sons for ever;" and that upon the same penalty with that of circumcision. To these he added many more on mount Sinai, Exod. xx.; all as the trials of their faith and obedience unto succeeding generations. How he hath dealt with his church under the New Testament we shall afterwards declare. In no state or condition, then, of the church did God ever accept of moral obedience without the observation of some instituted worship, accommodated in his wisdom unto its various states and conditions; and not only so, but, as we have seen, he hath made the observation of them, according unto his mind and appointment, the means of the trial of men's whole obedience, and the rule of the acceptance or rejection of them. And so it continues at this day, whatever be the thoughts of men about the worship which at present he requires.

Besides, God hath appointed that his worship shall be an *effectual means*, as to instruct us in the mysteries of his will and mind, so of communicating his love, mercy, and grace unto us; as also of that communion or intercourse with his holy Majesty, which he hath graciously granted unto us by Jesus Christ. And this, as it is sufficiently manifested in the Scriptures quoted in answer unto this question, so it is at large declared in the writings of those holy and good men who have explained the nature of the gospel ordinances; and therefore, in particular, we need not here insist much in the farther proof of it. Thus, Abraham was instructed in the nature of the covenant of grace by circumcision, Gen. xvii. 10, which is often explained in the Old Testament by applying it in particular to *the grace of conversion*, called the "circumcision of the heart," Deut. x. 16, xxx. 6, Jer. iv. 4; as also in the New Testament, Col. ii. 11. And by the passover were the people taught not only the mercy of their present deliverance, Exod. xii. 23, 24, but also to look for the Lamb of God who was to take away the sin of the world, John i. 29, the true Passover of the people of God, which was sacrificed for them, 1 Cor. v. 7. How our insition or implanting into Christ is represented and signified by our baptism, the apostle declares, Rom. vi. 3–5; as also our communion with him in his death, by the supper of the Lord, Matt. xxvi. 26, 27, 1 Cor. xi. 24, 25. And all these graces which they teach they also exhibit, and are the means of the communication of them unto believers. Moreover, the experience of all believers who have conscientiously waited upon God in their due observance may be produced in the confirmation of it. The instruction, edification, consolation, spiritual strength, courage, and resolution, which they have received in and by them, hath been witnessed unto in their lives and ends; and they to whom these things are not of the greatest importance do but in vain pretend a regard unto God in any thing whatever.

Furthermore; God hath appointed our duty in the observation of his instituted worship to be the means of our *glorifying him* in the world. Nor can we otherwise give glory to God but as we own his authority over us, and yield obedience to what he requires at our hands. And what we do herein is principally evident in those duties which lie under the eye and observation of men. Some duties of obedience there are which the world neither doth nor can discern in believers; such are their faith, inward holiness, purity of heart, heavenly-mindedness, sincere mortification of indwelling sin; some whose performance ought to be hid from them, as personal prayer and alms, Matt. vi. 2–6; some there are which are very liable to misconstruction amongst men, as zeal in many of the actings of it; but this conscientious observation of instituted worship, and therein avowing our subjection unto the authority of God in Christ, is that which the world may see and take notice of, and that which, unless in case of persecution, ought not to be hid from them, and that which they can have no pretence of scandal at: and therefore hath God appointed that by this means and way we shall honour and glorify him in the world; which if we neglect, we do evidently cast off all regard unto his concernments in this world. Herein it is that we manifest ourselves not to be ashamed of the gospel of Christ, of him and his words, which he so indispensably requireth at our hands: Mark viii. 38, "For," saith he, "whosoever shall be ashamed of me and of my words in this adulterous and sinful generation; of him also shall the Son of man be ashamed, when he cometh in the glory of his Father with the holy angels." Hereby do we keep the commandments of Christ, as his "friends," John xv. 14, for these peculiarly are his commands (and if we suffer for them, then we do most properly suffer as Christians, which is our glory), that, 1 Pet. iv. 14–16, "If ye be reproached for the name of Christ, happy are ye; for the spirit of glory and of God resteth upon you: on their part he is evil spoken of, but on your part he is glorified. But let none of you suffer as a murderer, or as a thief, or as an evil-doer, or as a busy-body in other men's matters. Yet if any man suffer as a Christian, let him not be ashamed; but let him glorify God on this behalf." And a happy and a blessed thing it is to suffer for the observation of the special commands of Christ.

Farther; to encourage us in our duty, the holy faithful God hath given us many *great and precious promises* that he will graciously afford unto us his especial, sanctifying, blessing presence, in our attendance on our worship according to his appointment; for as he promised of old that he would make glorious "the place of his feet," or abode among his people, Isa. lx. 13, — that he would meet them in his sanctuary, the place of his worship, and there dwell amongst them, and bless them, and be their God, Exod. xxix. 42–45, Deut. xiv. 23, 24, — so the Lord Jesus Christ hath promised his presence to the same ends and purposes, unto all them that assemble together in his name for the observation of the worship which in the gospel he hath appointed: Matt. xviii. 20, "For where two or three are gathered together in my name, there am I in the midst of them." And therein is the tabernacle of God, his gracious dwelling-place, with men, Rev. xxi. 3. Now, when God offereth unto us his presence, his gracious, blessing, sanctifying, and saving presence, and that in and by promises which shall never fail, what unspeakable guilt must we needs contract upon our souls if we neglect or despise the tenders of such grace!

Because we are apt to be slothful, and are slow of heart in admitting a due sense of spiritual things, that fall not in with the light and principles of nature, to stir us up unto a diligence in our attendance unto the will of God in this matter, he hath declared that he looks upon our obedience herein as our *whole loyalty* unto him in that *conjugal covenant* which he is pleased in Christ Jesus to take believers into with himself: Jer. iii. 14, 15, "Turn, O backsliding children, saith the Lord; for I am married unto you: and I will take you one of a city, and two of a family, and I will bring you unto Zion: and I will give you pastors according to mine heart, which shall feed you with knowledge and understanding." Coming unto Zion, in the worship of God, under the leading and conduct of pastors according to the heart of God, is our answering the relation wherein we stand unto him as he is married unto us; and thereupon he teacheth us that as a husband he is jealous of our discharge of our duty in this matter, accounting our neglect of his worship, or profanation of it by inventions and additions of our own, to be spiritual disloyalty, whoredom and adultery, which his soul abhorreth, for which he will cast off any church or people, and that for ever. See Exod. xx. 5; Deut. iv. 23, 24; Josh. xxiv. 19; Ezek. xvi. Whatever he will bear withal in his church, he will not bear with that which his jealousy is exercised about. If it transgress therein, he will give it a bill of divorce; which repudiated condition is the state of many churches in the world, however they please and boast themselves in their meretricious ornaments and practices.

To give yet farther strength unto all these considerations, that we may not only have rules and precepts, but examples also for our instruction, God hath given many signal instances of his *severity* against persons who, by ignorance, neglect, or regardlessness, have miscarried in not observing exactly his will and appointment in and about his worship. This was the case of Nadab and Abihu, the sons of Aaron, Lev. x. 1, 2; of Korah, Dathan, and Abiram, Num. xvi. 1–40; of the sons of Eli, — a sin not to be "expiated with sacrifice nor offering for ever," 1 Sam. ii. 27–34, iii. 14; of Uzza in putting the ark into a cart, when he should have borne it upon his shoulders, 1 Chron. xiii. 7–10; of Uzziah the king in offering incense contrary to God's institution, that duty being appropriated unto the priests of the posterity of Aaron, 2 Chron. xxvi. 16–21. These are sufficient intimations of what care and diligence we ought to use in attending unto what God hath appointed in his worship; and although now, under the New Testament, he doth not ordinarily proceed to the inflicting of temporal judgments in the like cases of neglect, yet he hath not wholly left us without instances of his putting forth tokens of his displeasure in temporal visitations on such miscarriages in his church: 1 Cor. xi. 30, "For this cause," saith the apostle, "many are weak and sickly among you, and many sleep." From all which it appears of what concernment it is unto the glory of God, and the salvation of our own souls, to attend diligently unto our duty in the strict and sincere observation of the worship of the gospel; for he lets us know that now a more severe punishment is substituted against such transgressions in the room of that which he so visibly inflicted under the Old Testament, Heb. x. 25–29.

Q. 16 *Is there yet any consideration that may stir up believers to a holy and religious care about the due observation of the institutions of the gospel?*

A. Yes; namely, that the great apostasy of the church in the last days, foretold in the Scripture, and which God threateneth to punish and revenge, consists principally in false worship and a departure from the institutions of Christ.—Rev. xiii. 4, 5, xvii. 1–5.

EXPLICATION. — That there is an apostasy of the church foretold in the book of the Revelation is acknowledged by all who with sincerity have inquired into the mind of God therein. The state of things at this day, and for many ages past in the world, sufficiently confirm that persuasion. And herein sundry things in general are obvious unto every sober consideration thereof:—

First, The horrible evils, troubles, and confusions that are to be brought into and upon the world thereby.

Secondly, The high guilt and provocation of God that is contained in it and doth accompany it.

Thirdly, The dreadful vengeance that God in his appointed time will take upon all the promoters and obstinate maintainers of it. These things are at large all of them foretold in the Revelation; and therein also the apostasy itself is set forth as the cause of all the plagues and destructions that, by the righteous judgment of God, are to be brought upon the world in these latter days. Now, as God doth earnestly call upon all that fear him not to intermeddle nor partake in the sins of the apostates, lest they should also partake in their judgments, — chap. xviii. 4, "I heard a voice from heaven, saying, Come out of her, my people, that ye be not partakers of her sins, and that ye receive not of her plagues;" — so he doth plainly declare wherein the apostasy and sin itself should principally consist; and that is in the corrupting and contaminating of the ordinances of his worship, or the introduction of false worship, joined with the persecution of them who refused to submit thereunto. For this cause is the sin itself set out under the name of "fornication" and "whoredom," and the church that maintains it is called "The mother of harlots," chap. xvii. 5. That by fornication and whoredom in the church, the adulterating of the worship of God, and the admission of false, self-invented worship in the room thereof, whereof God is jealous, is intended, the Scripture everywhere declares. It is easy, then, to gather of how great concernment unto us it is, especially in these latter days, wherein this so heinous and provoking sin is prevalent in the world, carefully to attend unto the safe, unerring rule of worship, and diligently to perform the duties that are required therein.

Q. 17 *Which are the principal institutions of the gospel to be observed in the worship of God?*

A. ªThe *calling*, gathering, and settling of churches, with their officers, as the seat and subject of all other solemn instituted worship; ᵇ*prayer*, with thanksgiving; ᶜ*singing* of psalms; ᵈ*preaching* the word; ᵉadministration of the *sacraments* of baptism and the supper of the Lord; ᶠ*discipline* and rule of the church collected and settled; most of which have also sundry particular duties relating unto them, and subservient unto their due observation.—ªMatt. xxviii. 19, 20; Acts ii. 41, 42; 1 Cor. xii. 28; Eph. iv. 11, 12; Matt. xviii. 17, 18; 1 Cor. iv. 17, vii. 17; Acts xiv. 23; Titus i. 5; 1 Tim. iii. 15.—ᵇ1 Tim. ii. 1; Acts vi. 4, xiii. 2, 3.—ᶜEph. v. 19; Col. iii. 16.—ᵈ2 Tim. iv. 2; Acts ii. 42; 1 Cor. xiv. 3; Acts vi. 4; Heb. xiii. 7.—ᵉMatt. xxviii. 19, xxvi. 26, 27; 1 Cor. xi. 23.—ᶠMatt. xviii. 17–19; Rom. xii. 6–8; Rev. ii., iii.

EXPLICATION. — These things, being all of them afterward to be spoken unto severally and apart, need not here any particular explication. They are the principal heads wherein gospel worship consisteth, and whereunto the particular duties of it may be reduced.

Q. 18 *Whereas sundry of these things are founded in the light and law of nature, as requisite unto all solemn worship, and are, moreover, commanded in the moral law, and explications of it in the Old Testament, how do you look upon them as evangelical institutions, to be observed principally on the authority of Jesus Christ?*

A. Neither their general suitableness unto the principles of right reason and the dictates of the light and law of nature, nor the practice of them in the worship of God under the Old Testament, does at all hinder them from depending on the mere institution of Jesus Christ, as to those especial ends of the glory of God in and by himself, and the edification of his church in the faith which is in him, whereunto he hath appointed them, nor as unto that especial manner of their performance which he requireth; in which respects they are to be observed on the account of his authority and command only.—Matt. xvii. 5, xxviii. 20; John xvi. 23, 24; Heb. iii. 4–6; Eph. i. 22, ii. 20–22; Heb. xii. 25.

EXPLICATION. — The principal thing we are to aim at, in the whole worship of God, is the discharge of that duty which we owe to Jesus Christ, the king and head of the church: Heb. iii. 6, "Christ as a son over his own house, whose house are we." 1 Tim. iii. 15, "That thou mayest know how thou oughtest to behave thyself in the house of God, which is the church of the living God." This we cannot do unless we consider his authority as the formal reason and cause of our observance of all that we do therein. If we perform any thing in the worship of God on any other account, it is no part of our obedience unto him, and so we can neither expect his grace to assist us, nor have we his promise to accept us therein; for that he hath annexed unto our doing and observing whatever he hath commanded, and that because he hath commanded us: Matt. xxviii. 20, "Teaching them to observe all things whatsoever I have commanded you; and, lo, I am with you alway, even unto the end of the world." This promised presence respects only the observance of his commands. Some men are apt to look on this authority of Christ as that which hath the least influence into what they do.

If in any of his institutions they find any thing that is suited or agreeable unto the light of nature, — as ecclesiastical societies, government of the church, and the like, they say, are, — they suppose and contend that that is the ground on which they are to be attended unto, and so are to be regulated accordingly. The interposition of his authority they will allow only in the *sacraments*, which have no light in reason or nature; so desirous are some to have as little to do with Christ as they can, even in the things that concern the worship of God! But it would be somewhat strange, that if what the Lord Christ hath appointed in his church to be observed in particular, in an especial manner, for especial ends of his own, hath in the general nature of it an agreement with what in like cases the light of nature seems to direct unto, therefore, his authority is not to be considered as the sole immediate reason of our performance of it. But it is evident, —

First, That our Lord Jesus Christ being the king and head of his church, the lord over the house of God, nothing is to be done therein but with respect unto his authority: Mat. xvii. 5, "This is my beloved Son, in whom I am well pleased; hear ye him." Eph. iv. 15, 16, "Speaking the truth in love, may grow up into him in all things, which is the head, even Christ: from whom the whole body fitly joined together and compacted by that which every joint supplieth, according to the effectual working in the measure of every part, maketh increase of the body unto the edifying of itself in love." Chap. ii. 20–22, "Ye are built upon the foundation of the apostles and prophets, Jesus Christ himself being the chief corner-stone; in whom all the building fitly framed together groweth unto an holy temple in the Lord: in whom ye also are built together for a habitation of God through the Spirit."

Secondly, And that, therefore, the suitableness of any thing to right reason or the light of nature is no ground for a church-observation of it, unless it be also appointed and commanded in especial by Jesus Christ.

Thirdly, That being so appointed and commanded, it becomes an especial institution of his, and as such is to be observed. So that in all things that are done, or to be done, or to be done, with respect unto the worship of God in the church, the authority of Christ is always principally to be considered, and every thing to be observed as commanded by him, without which consideration it hath no place in the worship of God.

Q. 19 *What is an instituted church of the gospel?*

A. A society of persons called out of the world, or their natural worldly state, by the administration of the word and Spirit, unto the obedience of the faith, or the knowledge and worship of God in Christ, joined together in a holy band, or by special agreement, for the exercise of the communion of saints, in the due observation of all the ordinances of the gospel. — Rom. i. 5, 6; 1 Cor. i. 2, iv. 15; Heb. iii. 1; James i. 18; Rev. i. 20; 1 Pet. ii. 5; Eph. ii. 20–22; 2 Cor. vi. 16–18.

EXPLICATION. — The church whose nature is here inquired after is not the *catholic* church of elect believers of all ages and seasons, from the beginning of the world unto the end thereof, nor of any one age, nor the *universality of professors* of the gospel; but a *particular church*, wherein, by the appointment of Christ, all the ordinances of the worship of God are to be observed and attended unto according to his will. For although it be required of them of whom a particular church is constituted that they be true believers, seeing that unless a man be born again he cannot enter into the kingdom of God, and so on that account they be members of the church catholic, as also that they make *visible profession* of faith and obedience unto Jesus Christ, yet moreover it is the will, command, and appointment of Christ, that they should be joined together in particular societies or churches, for the due observation of the ordinances of the gospel, which can alone be done in such assemblies. For as the members of the catholic church are not known unto one another merely on the account of that faith and union with Christ which make them so, — whence the whole society of them is, *as such, invisible* to the world, and themselves *visible* only on the account of their profession, and therefore cannot, merely as such, observe the ordinances of the gospel, which observation is their profession; — so the visible professors that are in the world, in any age, cannot at any time assemble together; which, from the nature of the thing itself, and the institution of Christ, is indispensably necessary for the celebration of sundry parts of that worship which he requires in his church: and therefore particular churches are themselves an ordinance of the New Testament, as the *national church* of the Jews was of old; for when God of old erected his worship, and enjoined the solemn observation of it, he also appointed a church as his institution for the due celebration of it. That was the people of Israel, solemnly taken into a church relation with him by covenant; wherein they took upon themselves to observe all the laws, and ordinances, and institutions of his worship: Exod. xx. 19, "Speak thou with us, and we will hear." Chap. xxiv. 3, "And Moses came and told the people all the words of the Lord, and all the judgments: and all the people answered with one voice, and said, All the words which the Lord hath said will we do." Deut. v. 27, "All that the Lord our God shall speak unto thee, we will hear it, and do it." And God accordingly appointed them ordinances to be observed by the whole congregation of them together, at the same time, in the same place: Exod. xxiii. 17, "Three times in the year all thy males shall appear before the Lord God." Deut. xvi. 16, "Three times in a year shall all thy males appear before the Lord thy God in the place which he shall choose."

Neither would God allow any stranger, any one not of the church so instituted by him, to celebrate any part of his instituted worship, until he was solemnly admitted into that church as a member thereof: Exod. xii. 47, 48, "All the congregation of Israel shall keep it. And when a stranger shall sojourn with thee, and will keep the passover to the Lord, let all his males be circumcised, and then let him come near and keep it; and he shall be as one that is born in the land: for no uncircumcised person shall eat thereof."

To the same end and purpose, when the knowledge of God was to be diffused all the world over by the preaching of the gospel, and believers of all nations under heaven were to be admitted unto the privilege of his worship, Eph. ii. 13–18, the national church of the Jews with all the ordinances of it being removed and taken away, the Lord Christ hath appointed *particular churches*, or united assemblies of believers, amongst and by whom he will have all his holy ordinances of worship celebrated. And this institution of his, at the first preaching of the gospel, was invariably and inviolably observed by all that took on them to be his disciples, without any one instance of questioning it to the contrary in the whole world, or the celebration of any ordinances of his worship amongst any persons, but only in such societies or particular churches. And there is sufficient evidence and warranty of this institution given us in the Scripture; for, —

First, They are appointed and approved by Christ: Matt. xviii. 15–20, "If thy brother shall trespass against thee, go and tell him his fault between thee and him alone: if he shall hear thee, thou hast gained thy brother. But if he will not hear thee, then take with thee one or two more, that in the mouth of two or three witnesses every word may be established. And if he shall neglect to hear them, tell it unto the church: but if he neglect to hear the church, let him be unto thee as a heathen man and a publican. Verily I say unto you, Whatsoever ye shall bind on earth shall be bound in heaven: and whatsoever ye shall loose on earth shall be loosed also in heaven. Again I say unto you, That if two of you shall agree on earth as touching any thing that they shall ask, it shall be done for them of my Father which is in heaven. For where two or three are gathered together in my name, there am I in the midst of them."

Such a church he supposeth and approveth as his disciples had relation unto, and as any one of them could have recourse unto, as a brother, in obedience to his commands and directions. This could not be the church of the Jews, neither in its whole body nor in any of its judicatories; for as at that time there was a solemn decree of excommunication against all and every one that should profess his name, — John ix. 22, "The Jews had agreed already, that if any man did confess that he was Christ, he should be put out of the synagogue," — which was executed accordingly upon the man that was born blind, verse 34, which utterly disabled them from making any use of this direction, command, or institution of his for the present; so afterward the chief business of the rulers of those assemblies, from the highest court of their sanhedrin to the meanest judicatory in their synagogues, was to persecute them and bring them unto death: Matt. x. 17, "They will deliver you up to the councils, and they will scourge you in their synagogues;" John xv. 20, 21. And it is not likely that the Lord Christ would send his disciples for direction and satisfaction in the weighty matters of their obedience unto him, and mutual love towards one another, unto them with whom they neither had, nor could, nor ought to have, any thing to do withal; and if they were intended, they were all already made as heathens and publicans, being cast out by them for refusing to hear them in their blasphemies and persecutions of Christ himself. Such a society, also, is plainly intended as whereunto Christ promiseth his presence by his Spirit, and whose righteous sentences he takes upon himself to ratify and confirm in heaven.

Moreover, such a church doth he direct unto as with which his disciples were to have familiar, brotherly, constant converse and communion, with whom they were so to be joined in society as to be owned or rejected by them according to their judgment; as is apparent in the practice enjoined unto them, and without relation whereunto no duty here appointed could be performed. As, therefore, the very name of the church and nature of the thing bespeak a society, so it is evident that no society but that of a particular church of the gospel can be here intended.

Secondly, These churches he calls his "candlesticks," Rev. i. 20, in allusion unto the candlesticks of the temple; which, being an institution of the Old Testament, doth directly declare these churches to be so under the New. And this he speaks in reference unto those seven principal churches of Asia, every one of which was a candlestick or an institution of his own.

Thirdly, In pursuit of this appointment of Christ, and by his authority, the apostles, so soon as any were converted unto the faith at Jerusalem, although the old national church-state of the Jews was yet continued, gathered them into a *church* or society for celebration of the ordinances of the gospel: Acts ii. 41, 42, "They that gladly received his word were baptized. And they continued stedfastly in the apostles' doctrine and fellowship, and in breaking of bread, and in prayers." Verse 47, "The Lord added to the church daily such as should be saved." And this company is expressly called "The church at Jerusalem," Acts viii. 1. This church, thus called and collected out of the church of the Jews, was the rule and pattern of the disposing of all the disciples of Christ into church-societies, in obedience unto his command, throughout the world, Acts xi. 26, xiv. 23, 27.

Fourthly, They took care for the forming, completing, and establishing them in *order* according to his will, under the rule of them given and granted unto them by himself for that purpose; all in a steady pursuit of the commands of Christ: Acts xiv. 23, "They ordained them elders in every church;" Titus i. 5, "For this cause left I thee in

Crete, that thou shouldest set in order the things that are wanting, and ordain elders in every city, as I had appointed thee;" 1 Cor. xii. 28; Eph. iv. 11, 12.

Fifthly, They do everywhere, in the name and authority of Christ, give unto these churches rules, directions, and precepts, for the due ordering of all things relating to the worship of God, and according to his mind, as we shall see afterward in particular; for, —

1. There is no charge given unto the officers, ministers, guides, or overseers that he hath appointed, but it is in reference unto the discharge of their duty in such churches. That ministers or officers are of Christ's appointment is expressly declared, Eph. iv. 11, 12, "He gave some, apostles; and some, prophets; and some, evangelists; and some, pastors and teachers; for the perfecting of the saints, for the work of the ministry, for the edifying of the body of Christ." 1 Cor. xii. 28, "God hath set some in the church, first apostles, secondarily prophets, thirdly teachers." These are of Christ's institution, but to what end? Why, as they were ordained in every church, Acts xiv. 23, Titus i. 5, so their whole charge is limited to the churches: Acts xx. 17, 18, 28, "He sent to Ephesus, and called the elders of the church, and said to them, Take heed therefore unto yourselves, and to all the flock, over the which the Holy Ghost hath made you overseers, to feed the church of God, which he hath purchased with his own blood;" 1 Pet. v. 1, 2, "the elders which are among you I exhort: feed the flock of God which is among you, taking the oversight thereof;" 1 Tim. iii. 15; Col. iv. 17, "And say to Archippus, Take heed to the ministry which thou hast received in the Lord, that thou fulfil it."

They were the churches of Christ wherein they ministered; which Christ, appointing them to take care of, manifests to be his own institution and appointment. And this is fully declared, Rev. ii., iii., where all the dealings of Christ with his angels, or ministers, are about their behaviour and deportment among his candlesticks, each of them, the candlestick whereunto he was related, or the particular churches that they had care of and presided in, the candlesticks being no less of the institution of Christ than the angels. And they were distinct particular churches, which had their distinct particular officers, whom he treated distinctly withal about his institutions and worship, especially about that of the state of the churches themselves, and their constitution according to his mind.

2. There is no instruction, exhortation, or reproof given unto any of the disciples of Christ after his ascension, in any of the books of the New Testament, but as they were collected into and were members of such particular churches. This will be evidenced in the many instances of those duties that shall afterwards be insisted on. And the Lord Christ hath not left that as a matter of liberty, choice, or conveniency, which he hath made the foundation of the due manner of the performance of all those duties whereby his disciples yield obedience unto his commands, to his glory in the world.

Sixthly, The principal writings of the apostles are *expressly* directed unto such churches, and all of them intentionally, 1 Cor. i. 1, 2; 2 Cor. i. 1; Gal. i. 1, 2; Phil. i. 1; Col. i. 1, 2, iv. 16; 1 Thess. i. 1; 2 Thess. i. 1; Eph. i. 1, compared with Acts xx. 17; 1 Pet. v. 2; — or unto such particular persons, giving directions for their behaviour and duty in such churches, 1 Tim. iii. 15; Titus i. 5. So that the great care of the apostles was about these churches, as the principal institution of Christ, and that whereon the due observance of all his other commands doth depend. Of what nature or sort these churches were shall be afterward evinced; we here only manifest their institution by the authority of Christ.

Seventhly, Much of the writings of the apostles, in those epistles directed to those churches, consists in rules, precepts, instructions, and exhortations for the guidance and preservation of them in purity and order, with their continuance in a condition of due obedience unto the Lord Christ. To this end do they so fully and largely acquaint the rulers and members of them with their mutual duty in that especial relation wherein they stand to each other; as also all persons in particular in what is required of them by virtue of their membership in any particular society; as may be seen at large in sundry of Paul's epistles. And to give more strength hereunto, our Lord Jesus Christ, in the revelation that he made of his mind and will personally after his ascension into heaven, insisted principally about the condition, order, and preservation of particular churches, not taking notice of any of his disciples not belonging to them or joined with them. These he warns, reproves, instructs, threatens, commands; all in order to their walking before him in the condition of particular churches, Rev. ii. and iii. at large.

Besides, as he hath appointed them to be the seat and subject of all his ordinances, having granted the right of them unto them alone, 1 Tim. iii. 15, intrusting them with the exercise of that authority which he puts forth in the rule of his disciples in this world, he hath also appointed the most holy institution of his supper to denote and express that union and communion which the members of each of these churches have by his ordinance among themselves: 1 Cor. x. 16, 17, "The cup of blessing which we bless, is it not the communion of the blood of Christ? The bread which we break, is it not the communion of the body of Christ? For we being many are one bread, and one body: for we are all partakers of that one bread." And also he gives out unto them the gifts and graces of his Spirit, to make every one of them meet for and useful in that place which he holds in such churches; as the apostle discourseth at large, 1 Cor. xii. 15–26; Col. ii. 19; Eph. iv. 16. It is manifest, then, that no ordinance of Christ is appointed to be observed by his disciples, no communication of the gifts of the Holy Ghost is promised to them, no especial duty is required of them, but with respect unto these churches of his institution.

In the answer to this question four things are declared tending to the explication of the nature of a particular church or churches:— 1. The *subject-matter* of them, or the persons whereof such a church doth or ought to consist. 2. The *means* whereby they are brought into a condition capable of such an estate, or qualified for it. 3. The *general ends* of their calling. 4. The *especial means* whereby they are constituted a church; which last will be spoken unto in the next question.

For the first, all men are by nature the children of wrath, and do belong unto the world, which is the kingdom of Satan, and are under the power of darkness, as the Scripture everywhere declares. In this state men are not subjects of the kingdom of Christ, nor meet to become members of his church.

Out of this condition they cannot deliver themselves. They have neither will unto it nor power for it; but they are called out of it. This calling is that which effectually delivers them from the kingdom of Satan, and translates them into the kingdom of Christ. And this work or effect, the Scripture, on several accounts, variously expresseth; sometimes by *regeneration*, or a new birth; sometimes by *conversion*, or turning unto God; sometimes by *vivification*, or quickening from the dead; sometimes from *illumination*, or opening the eyes of the blind; — all which are carried on by *sanctification* in holiness, and attended with justification and adoption. And as these are all distinct in themselves, having several formal reasons of them, so they all concur to complete that effectual vocation or calling that is required to constitute persons members of the church. For besides that this is signified by the typical holiness of the church of old, into the room whereof real holiness was to succeed under the New Testament, — Exod. xix. 6; Ps. xxiv. 3–6, xv. 1, 2; Isa. xxxv. 8, 9, liv. 13, 14, lx. 21; 1 Pet. ii. 9, — our Lord Jesus Christ hath laid it down as an everlasting rule, that "except a man be born again, he cannot enter the kingdom of God," John iii. 3, 5, requiring regeneration as an indispensable condition in a member of his church, a subject of his kingdom: for his temple is now to be built of living stones, 1 Pet. ii. 5, — men spiritual and savingly quickened from their death in sin, and by the Holy Ghost, whereof they are partakers, made a meet habitation of God, Eph. ii. 21, 22; 1 Cor. iii. 16; 2 Cor. vi. 16; which receiving vital supplies from Christ its head, increaseth in faith and holiness, edifying itself in love, Eph. iv. 15, 16. And as the apostles in their writings do ascribe unto all the churches, and the members of them, a participation in this effectual vocation, affirming that they are "saints, called, sanctified, justified," and accepted with God in Christ, — Rom. i. 5, 6; 1 Cor. i. 2, iv. 15; Heb. iii. 1; James i. 18; 1 Pet. ii. 5; 2 Cor. vi. 17, 18; 1 Cor. vi. 11, — so many of the duties that are required of them in that relation and condition are such as none can perform unto the glory of God, their own benefit, and the edification of others (the ends of all obedience), unless they are partakers of this effectual calling, 1 Cor. x. 16, 17, xii. 12; Eph. iv. 16. And hereunto that these churches, and the members of them, are not only commanded to separate themselves, as to their worship of God, from the world, — that is, men in their worldly state and condition, — but are also required, when any amongst them transgress against the rules and laws of this holy calling above described, to cast them out of their society and communion, 1 Cor. v. 13. From all which it appears who are the subject-matter of these churches of Christ; as also, secondly, the means whereby they come to be so, — namely, the administration of the Spirit and word of Christ; and, thirdly, the general ends of their calling, which are all spoken to in this answer.

Q. 20 *By what means do persons so called become a church of Christ?*

A. They are constituted a church, and interested in the rights, power, and privileges of a gospel church, by the will, promise, authority, and law of Jesus Christ, upon their own voluntary consent and engagement to walk together in the due subjection of their souls and consciences unto his authority, as their king, priest, and prophet, and in a holy observation of all his commands, ordinances, and appointments.—Matt. xviii. 20, xxviii. 19, 20; Acts ii. 41, 42; Exod. xxiv. 3; Deut. v. 27; Ps. cx. 3; Isa. xliv. 5, lix. 21; Eph. iv. 7–10; 2 Cor. viii. 5.

EXPLICATION. — That the Lord Christ hath constituted such a church-state as that which we inquire about hath been proved already. Unto a church so constituted he hath also, by his word and promise, annexed all those privileges and powers which we find a church to be intrusted withal. This he hath done by the standing and unalterable law of the gospel, which is the charter of their spiritual society and incorporation. Neither are nor can any persons be interested in the rights of a church any otherwise but by virtue of this law and constitution. This, therefore, is first to be laid down, that the sole moral foundation of that church-state which we inquire after is laid in the word, law, and appointment of Christ. He alone hath authority to erect such a society; he is the builder of this house as well as the lord over it, Heb. iii. 3–6. Neither without it can all the authority of men in the world appoint such a state or erect a church; and all acceptable actings of men herein are no other but acts of pure obedience unto Christ.

Furthermore, we have declared that the Lord Christ, by the dispensation of his word and Spirit, doth prepare and fit men to be subjects of his kingdom, members of his church. The work of sending forth the means of the conversion of the souls of men, of translating them from the power of darkness into light, he hath taken upon himself, and doth effectually accomplish it in every generation. And by this means he builds his church, for unto all persons so called he gives command that they shall do and observe whatever he hath appointed them to do, Matt. xxviii. 20; in particular, that they profess their subjection to him, and their obedience, in joining themselves in that state wherein they may be enabled to observe all his other laws and institutions, with the whole worship of God required therein. Being converted unto God by his word and Spirit, they are to consider how they may now obey the Lord Christ in all things. Amongst his commands, this of joining themselves in church-societies, wherein he hath promised his presence with them, Matt. xxviii. 20, — that is, to dwell amongst them by his word and Spirit, Isa. lix. 21, — is the very first. This, by virtue of that command and promise of his, they are warranted and enabled to do; nor do they need any other warrant. The authority of Christ is sufficient to bear men out in the discharge of their duty to him. Being then made willing and ready in the day of his power, Ps. cx. 3, they consent, choose, and agree to walk together in the observation of all his commands. And hereby do they become a church; for their becoming a church is an act of their willing obedience unto Christ. This is an act of their wills, guided by rule; for this also is necessary, that they proceed herein according to the rules of his appointment, afterward to be unfolded. And herein, upon their obedience unto the commands of Christ, and faith in his promises, do believers, by virtue of his law and constitution, become a gospel church, and are really and truly interested in all the power, rights, and privileges that are granted unto any church of Christ; for in this obedience they do these two things, which alone he requires in any persons for the obtaining of an interest in these privileges:— First, They *confess* him, his person, his authority, his law, his grace; secondly, They take upon themselves the observance of all his commands.

Thus did God take the children of Israel into a church-state of old. He proposed unto them the church-obedience that he required of them, and they voluntarily and freely took upon themselves the performance of it: Exod. xxiv. 3, "And Moses came and told the people all the words of the Lord, and all the judgments: and all the people answered with one voice, and said, All the words which the Lord hath said will we do:" so Deut. v. 27. And hereby they had their solemn admission into their church-state and relation unto God. And the like course they took whenever there was need of renewing of their engagements: Josh. xxiv. 18–22, "And the people said, We will serve the Lord; for he is our God. And Joshua said unto the people, Ye are witnesses against yourselves that ye have chosen the Lord, to serve him. And they said, We are witnesses." This was the covenant that was between God and that people, which was solemnly renewed so often as the church was eminently reformed. Now, although the outward solemnity and ceremonies of this covenant were peculiar unto that people, yet as to the substance and nature of it, in a sacred consent for the performance of all those duties towards God and one another which the nature and edification of a church do require, it belongs to every church as such, even under the gospel.

And this is the way whereby believers, or the disciples of Christ, do enter into this state, the formal constituting cause of any church, this account doth the apostle give of the churches of the Macedonians: 2 Cor. viii. 5, "And this they did, not as we hoped, but first gave their own selves to the

Lord, and unto us by the will of God," before the performance of other duties; and in order thereunto, they first gave themselves to the Lord Jesus Christ, or took upon themselves the observance of his commands and institutions, which is the intendment of that expression. Among these commands one was, that they should give up themselves to the apostles' doctrine, rule, and government, in the order by Christ prescribed, — that is, in church-order. This, therefore, they did by *the will of God*, according to his will and appointment. This description doth the apostle give of the way whereby the believers of Macedonia were brought into churches. It was by their own obedience unto the will of God; consenting, agreeing, and taking upon themselves the observation of all the commands and institutions of Christ, according to the direction and guidance of the apostles. So did the believers at Jerusalem, Acts ii. 41, 42. Being converted by the word, and making profession of that conversion in their baptism, they gave up themselves to a steadfast continuance in the observation of all other ordinances of the gospel.

Besides, the church is a house, a temple, — the "house of God," 1 Tim. iii. 15; the "house of Christ," Heb. iii. 6; the "temple of the Lord," Eph. ii. 21, 22. Believers, singly considered, are "stones, living stones," 1 Pet. ii. 5. Now, how shall these "living stones" come to be a house, a temple? Can it be by occasional occurrences, civil cohabitation in political precincts, usage, or custom of assembling for some parts of worship in any place? These things will never frame them into a house or temple. This can be no otherwise done but by their own voluntary consent and disposition: Eph. ii. 19–22, "Ye are fellow-citizens with the saints, and of the household of God; and are built upon the foundation of the apostles and prophets, Jesus Christ himself being the chief corner-stone; in whom all the building fitly framed together groweth unto a holy temple in the Lord: in whom ye also are builded together for an habitation of God through the Spirit." Chap. iv. 16, "From whom the whole body fitly joined together and compacted by that which every joint supplieth, according to the effectual working in the measure of every part, maketh increase of the body unto the edifying of itself in love." From these and sundry other places it is manifest that the way and means of believers' coalition into a church-state is their own obedience of faith, acting itself in a joint voluntary consent to walk together in a holy observation of the commands of Christ; whence the being and union of a particular church is given unto any convenient number of them by his law and constitution.

Q. 21 *Seeing the church is a society or spiritual incorporation of persons under rule, government, or discipline, declare who or what are the rulers, governors, or officers therein under Jesus Christ?*

A. They have been of two sorts: 1. *Extraordinary*, appointed for a season only; and, 2. *Ordinary*, to continue unto the end of the world.

Q. 22 *Who are the extraordinary officers, or rulers, or ministers of the church, appointed to serve the Lord Jesus Christ therein for a season only?*

A. ªThe apostles of our Lord Jesus Christ, with ᵇthe evangelists and prophets, endowed with extraordinary gifts of the Holy Ghost, associated with them and employed by them in their works and ministry.—ªMatt. x. 2–4; Acts i. 26; 1 Cor. xii.

28; Eph. iv. 11.—ᵇLuke x. 1; 2 Tim. iv. 5; Titus i. 5; Acts xi. 27, 28, xxi. 9–11; 2 Cor. i. 1.

EXPLICATION. — That the church is a spiritual corporation, attended with rule and government, is evident from the nature of the thing itself and testimonies of Scripture. Only, as the kingdom of Christ is not of this world or worldly, so this rule and government of the church is not merely external and secular, but spiritual. Neither doth this rule at all belong unto it merely as *materially* considered, in men yielding obedience unto the call which is the foundation of the church; nor *absolutely*, as it is formally constituted a church by the consent and agreement described; but, moreover, it is required that it be *organically* complete, with officers or rulers. Now, to the constitution of such a society or corporation there is required, —

First, That the persons whereof it is constituted do *consent* together into it for the attaining of the ends which they design. Without this no society of any kind can exist. This is the form of men's coalescency into societies; and that there is in the church such consent and agreement hath been showed.

Secondly, That there be rules or laws for the guidance and direction of all the members of the society, in order to their pursuit of the proper ends of it. That such rules or laws are given and prescribed by the Lord Christ unto the church will afterward appear, in our consideration of them in particular; so that the church is a society of men walking according unto rule or law for the attaining of the ends of the society.

Thirdly, That there be authority instituted to see to the due observation of these rules and laws of the society, which consists in this:— 1. That some be appointed to rule and govern in the church; 2.

Others to obey and be ruled or governed; both according to the laws of the society, and not otherwise. And both these are eminently found in this church-state, as we shall see in the ensuing questions, with their answers and explications.

Now, that these officers or rulers should be of two sorts, both the nature of the thing itself required and so hath our Lord Jesus Christ appointed; for when the church was first to be called, gathered, and erected, it was necessary that some persons should be extraordinarily employed in that work, for ordinary officers antecedent unto the calling and erection of the church there could be none. And, therefore, these persons were in an extraordinary manner endowed with all the power which afterward was to reside in the churches themselves; and, moreover, with that which was peculiarly needful unto the discharge and performance of that special duty and work that they were appointed unto. But when churches were called, gathered, erected, and settled for continuance, there was need of officers suited to their state and condition, called in an ordinary way, — that is, in a way appointed for continuance unto the end of the world; and to be employed in the ordinary work of the church, — that is, the duties of it were constantly incumbent on it by virtue of the command and appointment of Christ.

Q. 23 *Who are the ordinary officers or ministers of Christ in the church, to be always continued therein?*

A. Those whom the Scripture calls pastors and teachers, bishops, elders, and guides.—Acts xiv. 23, xx. 17, 28; 1 Cor. xii. 28; Eph. iv. 11; Phil. i. 1; 1 Tim. iii. 1, 2, v. 17; Titus i. 5, 7; Heb. xiii. 7, 17; 1 Pet. v. 1.

EXPLICATION. — Several names are, on several accounts, partly designing their authority, partly their duty, and partly the manner of their discharge thereof, assigned in the Scripture to the ordinary ministers of the churches. Sometimes they are called "pastors and teachers," Eph. iv. 11; 1 Cor. xii. 28; — sometimes "bishops" or "overseers," Phil. i. 1; Acts xx. 28; — sometimes "elders," Titus i. 5; 1 Pet. v. 1; 1 Tim. v. 17; Acts xiv. 23, xx. 17; — sometimes "guides," Heb. xiii. 7, 17. By all which names, and sundry others whereby they are expressed, the same sort, order, and degree of persons is intended. Nor is any one of these names applied or accommodated unto any, but all the rest are also in like manner; so that he who is a pastor or a teacher is also a bishop or overseer, a presbyter or elder, a guide or ruler, a minister, a servant of the church for the Lord's sake. And of all other names assigned to the ministers of the church, that of bishop can least of all be thought to have designed any special order or degree of pre-eminence amongst them; for whereas it is but four times, or in four places, used in the New Testament as denoting any officers of the church, in each of them it is manifest that those expressed by the other names of elders and ministers are intended. So, Acts xx. 28, the bishops are the elders of the particular church of Ephesus, verse 17. Phil. i. 1, there were many bishops in that one particular church, who had only deacons joined with them; that is, they were the elders of it, Titus i. 7. The bishops were the elders to be ordained, verse 5; which persons are also directly intended, 1 Tim. iii. 2, as is evident from the coincidence of the directions given by the apostles about them, and the immediate adjoining of deacons unto them, verse

8; so that no name could be fixed on with less probability, to assert from it a special supreme order or degree of men in the ministry, than this of bishops. Neither is there any mention in any place of Scripture of any such pre-eminence of one sort of these church-officers or ministers over another, not in particular in those places where the officers of the church are in an especial manner enumerated, as 1 Cor. xii. 28; Eph. iv. 11; Rom. xii. 5–8. Nor is there any mention of any special office that should be peculiar unto such officers; or of any gifts or qualifications that should be required in them; or of any special way of calling or setting apart to their office; nor of any kind of church that they should relate unto, different from the churches that other elders or pastors do minister in; nor of any special rule or direction for their trial; nor any commands for obedience unto them but what are common to all ministers of the churches of Christ duly discharging their trust and performing their duty; no intimation is given unto either elders or ministers to obey them, or directions how to respect them, nor unto them how to behave themselves toward them: but all these things are spoken and delivered promiscuously and equally concerning all ministers of the gospel. It is evident, then, that these appellations do not belong unto one sort of ministers, not more than another. And for what is pleaded by some from the example of Timothy and Titus, it is said that when any persons can prove themselves to be evangelists, 2 Tim. iv. 5, to be called unto their office upon antecedent prophecy, 1 Tim. i. 18, and to be sent by the apostles, and in an especial manner to be directed by them in some employment for a season, which they are not ordinarily to attend unto, Titus i. 5, iii. 12, it will be granted that they have another duty and office committed unto them than those who are only bishops or elders in the Scripture.

Q. 24 *What are the principal differences between these two sorts of officers or rulers in the church, extraordinary and ordinary?*

A. ᵃThe former were called to their office immediately by Jesus Christ in his own person, or revelation made by the Holy Ghost in his name to that purpose; the latter by the suffrage, choice, and appointment of the church itself. ᵇThe former, both in their office and work, were independent on, and antecedent unto, all or any churches, whose calling and gathering depended on their office as its consequent and effect; the latter, in both, consequent unto the calling, gathering, and constituting of the churches themselves, as an effect thereof, in their tendency unto completeness and perfection. ᶜThe authority of the former being communicated unto them immediately by Jesus Christ, without any intervenient actings of any church, extended itself equally unto all churches whatever; that of the latter being derived unto them from Christ by the election and designation of the church, is in the exercise of it confined unto that church wherein and whereby it is so derived unto them. ᵈThey differ also in the gifts, which were suited unto their several distinct works and employments.—ᵃMatt. x. 1; Luke x. 1; Gal. i. 1; Acts i. 26, vi. 3, xiv. 23.—ᵇJohn xx. 21–23; Gal. i. 1; Eph. ii. 20; Rev. xxi. 14; Acts xiv. 23; Titus i. 5, 7.—ᶜMatt. xxviii. 18–20; 2 Cor. xi. 28; Acts xx. 28; 1 Pet. v. 2; Col. iv. 17.—ᵈ1 Cor. xii. 28–33.

The answer hereunto is such as needs no farther explication.

Q. 25 *What is required unto the due constitution of an elder, pastor, or teacher of the church?*

A. ᵃThat he be furnished with the gifts of the Holy Spirit for the edification of the church, and the evangelical discharge of the work of the ministry; ᵇthat he be unblamable, holy, and exemplary in his conversation; ᶜthat he have a willing mind to give himself unto the Lord in the work of the ministry; ᵈthat he be called and chosen by the suffrage and consent of the church; ᵉthat he be solemnly set apart by fasting and prayer, and imposition of hands, unto his work and ministry. — ᵃEph. iv. 7, 8, 11–13. — ᵇTitus i. 7–9; 1 Tim. iii. 2–7. — ᶜ1 Pet. v. 1–3. — ᵈActs xiv. 23. — ᵉActs xiii. 2, 3; 1 Tim. iv. 14, v. 22.

EXPLICATION. — Five things are here said to be required unto the due and solemn constitution of a minister, guide, elder, pastor, or teacher of the church, which, as they do all equally belong unto the essence of the call, so they are all indispensably necessary unto him that would be accounted to have taken that office upon him according to the mind of Christ; and they that are plainly expressed in the Scripture.

The first is, That they be furnished with the *gifts* of the Holy Ghost for the discharge of the ministry. The communication of the gifts of the Holy Ghost is the foundation of the ministry, as the apostle declares, Eph. iv. 7, 8, , 11–13, "But unto every one of us is given grace according to the measure of the gift of Christ. Wherefore he saith, When he ascended up on high, he led captivity captive, and gave gifts unto men. And he gave some, apostles; and some prophets; and some, evangelists; and some, pastors and teachers; for the perfecting of the saints, for the work of the ministry, for the edifying of the body of Christ: till we all come in the unity of the faith, and of the knowledge of the Son of God, unto a perfect man." And if this were not continued, if the Lord Christ did not continue to give gifts unto men for that end, the ministry must and would cease in the church, and all church order and administrations thereon. The exercise, also, of the gifts is required in all them that are called unto sacred offices: 1 Tim. iv. 14, "Neglect not the gift that is in thee." Hence, persons destitute of these gifts of the Spirit, as they cannot in a due manner discharge any one duty of the ministry, so, wanting an interest in that which is the foundation of the office, are not esteemed of God as ministers at all, whatever their outward call may be: Hos. iv. 6, "Because thou hast rejected knowledge, I will also reject thee, that thou shalt be no priest to me."

Secondly, Their unblamableness and holiness of conversation is previously required in them that are to be set apart unto the ministry. This the apostle expressly declares, and lays down many particular instances whereby it is to be tried: Titus i. 7–9, "For a bishop must be blameless, as the steward of God; not self-willed, not soon angry, not given to wine, no striker, not given to filthy lucre; but a lover of hospitality, a lover of good men, sober, just, holy, temperate; holding fast the faithful word as he hath been taught, that he may be able by sound doctrine both to exhort and convince the gainsayers." 1 Tim. iii. 2–7, "A bishop must be blameless, the husband of one wife, vigilant, sober, of good behaviour, given to hospitality, apt to teach; not given to wine, no striker, not greedy of filthy lucre; but patient, not a brawler, not covetous; one that ruleth well his own house, having his children in subjection with all gravity; (for if a man know not how to rule his own house, how shall he take care of the church of God?) not a novice, lest being lifted up with pride he fall into the condemnation of the devil. Moreover he must have a good report of them which are without; lest he fall into reproach and the snare of the devil." Not that the particulars here mentioned by the apostle are only to be considered in the conversation of the person to be called to the ministry, but that, in a universal holy conversation, these things he requires that he should be eminent in amongst believers, as those which have an especial respect to his work and office. And a failure in any of them is a just cause or reason to debar any person from obtaining a part and lot in this matter; for whereas the especial end of the ministry is to promote and further faith and holiness in the church by the edification of it, how unreasonable a thing would it be if men should be admitted unto the work of it who in their own persons were strangers both unto faith and holiness! And herein are the elders of the churches seriously to exercise themselves unto God, that they may be an example unto the flock, in a universal labouring after conformity in their lives unto the great bishop and pastor of the church, our Lord Jesus Christ.

Thirdly, It is required that such a person have a *willing mind* to give up himself unto God in this work: 1 Pet. v. 1–3, "The elders which are among you, I exhort: feed the flock of God which is among you, taking the oversight thereof, not by constraint, but willingly; not for filthy lucre, but of a ready mind; neither as being lords over God's heritage, but being ensamples to the flock." Willingness and readiness of mind are the things here required as a previous qualification unto any man's susception of this office; and two things doth the apostle declare to be contrary hereunto: —

1. The undertaking of it by *constraint*, which compriseth every antecedent external impression upon the mind of the undertaker; such are personal outward necessities, compulsions of friends and relations, want of other ways of subsistence in the world, — which, and the like, are condemned by the apostle as bringing some constraint on the mind, which on other accounts ought to be free and willing; as also, all tergiversation and backwardness in persons duly qualified and called, on the consideration of difficulties, temptations, straits, persecutions, is here condemned.

2. An eye and regard unto *filthy lucre* or profit in the world is proposed as opposite unto the readiness of mind which is required in them that are called to this work. An aim in this employment for men by it to advantage themselves in the outward things of this world, — without which it is evident that the whole work and office would lie neglected by the most of them who now would be accounted partakers of it, — is openly here condemned by the apostle.

Fourthly, *Election*, by the suffrage and consent of the church, is required unto the calling of a pastor or teacher; so that without it formally or virtually given or obtained, the call, however otherwise carried on or solemnized, is irregular and defective. There are but two places in the New Testament where there is mention of the manner whereby any are called in an ordinary way unto any ministry in the church, and in both of them there is mention of their election by the community of the church; and in both of them the apostles themselves presided with a fulness of church-power, and yet would not deprive the churches of that which was their liberty and privilege. The first of these is Acts vi., where all the apostles together, to give a rule unto the future proceeding of all churches in the constitution of officers amongst them, do appoint the multitude of the disciples or community of the church, to look out from among themselves, or to choose the persons that were to be set apart therein unto their office; which they did accordingly: Verses 2, 3, 5, "Then the twelve called the multitude of the disciples unto them, and said, It is not reason that we should leave the word of God, and serve tables. Wherefore, brethren, look ye out among you seven men of honest report, full of the Holy Ghost and wisdom. And the saying pleased the whole multitude: and they chose Stephen," etc. This was done when only deacons were to be ordained, in whom the interest and concernment of the church is not to be compared with that which it hath in its pastors, teachers, and elders. The same is mentioned again, Acts xiv. 23, where Paul and Barnabas are said to ordain elders in the churches by their election and suffrage; for the word there used will admit of no other sense, however it be ambiguously expressed in our translation. Neither can any instance be given of the use of that word, applied unto the communication of any office or power to any person or persons in an assembly, wherein it denoteth any other action but the suffrage of the multitude; and this it doth constantly in all writers in the Greek tongue. And hence it was that this right and privilege of the church, in choosing of those who are to be set over them in the work of the Lord, was a long time preserved inviolate in the primitive churches, as the ancients do abundantly testify.

Yea, the show and appearance of it could never be utterly thrust out of the world, but is still retained in those churches which yet reject the thing itself. And this institution of our Lord Jesus Christ by his apostles is suited to the nature of the church, and of the authority that he hath appointed to abide therein; for, as we have showed before, persons become a church by their own voluntary consent. Christ makes his subjects willing, not slaves; his rule over them is by his grace in their own wills, and he will have them every way free in their obedience. A church-state is an estate of absolute liberty under Christ, not for men to do what they will, but for men to do their duty freely, without compulsion. Now, nothing is more contrary to this liberty than to have their guides, rulers, and overseers imposed on them without their consent. Besides, the body of the church is obliged to discharge its duty towards Christ in every institution of his; which herein they cannot, if they have not their free consent in the choice of their pastors or elders, but are considered as mute persons or brute creatures. Neither is there any other ordinary way of communicating authority unto any in the church, but by the voluntary submission and subjection of the church itself unto them; for as all other imaginable ways may fail, and have done so, where they have been trusted unto, so they are irrational and unscriptural as to their being a means of the delegation of any power whatever.

Fifthly, Unto this election succeeds the solemn setting apart of them that are chosen by the church unto this work and ministry, by fasting, prayer, and imposition of the hands of the presbytery, before constituted in the church wherein any person is so to be set apart.

Q. 26 *May a person be called to, or be employed in, a part only of the office or work of the ministry; or may he hold the relation and exercise the duty of an elder or minister unto more churches than one at the same time?*

A. Neither of these has either warrant or precedent in the Scripture; nor is the first of them consistent with the authority of the ministry, nor the latter with the duty thereof, nor either of them with the nature of that relation which is between the elders and the church.—Acts xiv. 23; 1 Pet. v. 2; Acts xx. 28.

EXPLICATION. — There are two parts of this question and answer, to be spoken unto severally. The first is concerning a person to be called or employed in any church in a part only of the office or work of the ministry; — as suppose a man should be called or chosen by the church to administer the sacraments, but not to attend to the work of preaching, or unto the rule or guidance of the church; or, in like manner, unto any other part or parcel of the work of the ministry, with an exemption of other duties from his charge or care. If this be done by consent and agreement, for any time or season, it is unwarrantable and disorderly (what may be done occasionally upon an emergency, or in case of weakness or disability befalling any elder as to the discharge of any part of his duty, is not here inquired after); for, —

First, If the person so called or employed have received gifts fitting him for the whole work of the ministry, the exercise of them is not to be restrained by any consent or agreement, seeing they are given for the edification of the church to be traded withal: 1 Cor. xii. 7, "The manifestation of the Spirit is given to every man to profit withal;"

and this he who hath received such gifts is bound to attend unto and pursue.

Secondly, If he have not received such gifts as completely to enable him unto the discharge of the whole work of the ministry in the church wherein he is to administer, it is not lawful for the church to call him unto that work wherein the Lord Christ hath not gone before them in qualifying him for it; yea, to do so would be most irregular, for the whole power of the church consists in its attendance unto the rule given unto it: and therefore the office and work of the ministry being constituted by the law of Christ, it is not in the power of the church to enlarge or straiten the power or duty of any one that is called unto the office thereof. Neither can or ought any person that is called unto the work of the ministry to give his consent to the restraint of the exercise of that gift that he hath received, in a due and orderly manner, nor to the abridgment of the authority which the Lord Christ hath committed unto the ministers of the gospel.

As it is incumbent upon them to take care to preserve their whole authority, and to discharge their whole duty, so it follows that arbitrary constitutions of this nature are irregular, and would bring in confusion into churches.

The second part of the question is concerning the relation of the same person to more churches than one at the same time, and his undertaking to discharge the duty of his relation unto them, as elder or minister. And this also is irregular and unwarrantable. Now, a man may hold the relation of an elder, pastor, or minister unto more churches than one, two ways:— 1. Formally and directly, by an equal formal interest in them, undertaking the pastoral charge equally and alike of them, being called alike to them, and accepting of such a relation. 2. Virtually, when, by virtue of his relation unto one church, he puts forth his power or authority in ministerial acts in or towards another. The first way is unlawful, and destructive both of the office and duty of a pastor; for as elders are ordained in and unto the churches respectively that they are to take care of, Acts xiv. 23, Titus i. 5, and their office-power consists in a relation unto the church that they are set over, so they are commanded to attend unto the service of the churches wherein and whereunto they are so ordained, Acts xx. 28, 1 Pet. v. 2, and that with all diligence, care, and watchfulness, as those that must give an account, Heb. xiii. 17, which no man is able to do towards more churches than one, the same duty being at all times to be performed towards all. And because the whole authority of the elders, pastors, or bishops of churches, is ministerial, 1 Cor. iv. 1, consisting in a power of acting upon the command of Christ, they are bound in their own persons to the discharge of their duty and office, without the least pretence of authority to delegate another, or others, to act their part or to do their duty; which would be an effect of autocratical authority, and not of obedience or ministry. The latter way, also, of relation unto many churches is unwarrantable: for, — 1. It hath no *warrant* in the Scripture; no law or constitution of Christ or his apostles can be produced to give it countenance; but elders were ordained to their own churches, and commanded to attend unto them. 2. No *rule* is given unto any elders how they should behave themselves in reference unto more churches than one, in the exercise of their ministerial power, as there are rules given unto every one for the discharge of that duty in the church whereunto he is related. 3. There is no *example* to give it countenance recorded in the Scripture. 4. The authority to be put forth hath no foundation. (1.) Not in the *gifts* they have received; for the ministerial power is not an absolute ability or faculty of doing what a man is able, but a *right*, whereby a man hath power to do that rightly and lawfully which before he could not do. This, gifts will not give to any; for if they did, they would do it to all that have received them. (2.) Not in their *election*; for they are chosen in and by that church whereunto they stand in especial relation, whose choice cannot give ministerial power over any but themselves. (3.) Not in their *setting apart* by fasting, prayer, and imposition of hands; for this is only unto that office-work and power whereunto they are chosen. They are not chosen for one end, and set apart for another. (4.) Not from the communion of churches; for that gives no new power, but only a due exercise of that which was before received.

Q. 27 *What are the principal duties of the pastors or teachers of the church?*

A. [a]To be examples unto the flock in faith, love, knowledge, meekness, patience, readiness to suffer for the name and gospel of Christ, with constancy therein; [b]to watch for the souls and take care of all the spiritual concernments of the whole flock committed to them; [c]to preach the word diligently, dividing it aright; [d]to preserve and contend for the truth; [e]to administer all the ordinances of the gospel duly and orderly; [f]to stir up and exercise the gifts they have received in the discharge of their whole work and administration of all ordinances; [g]to instruct, admonish, cherish, and comfort all the members of the church, as their conditions, occasions, and necessities do require; ʰto attend with diligence, skill, and wisdom unto the discharge of that authority which in the rule of the church is committed unto them.—ᵃ1 Tim. iii. 1–7, iv. 12; 2 Tim. ii. 3; Col. i. 24; Phil. ii. 17, iii. 17.—ᵇHeb. xiii. 17; Acts xx. 28.—ᶜ2 Tim. ii. 15, iv. 2; Rom. xii. 6–8.—ᵈ1 Tim. vi. 20; Acts xx. 28; Jude 3.—ᵉ1 Cor. iv. 1, 2; 1 Tim. iii. 15.—ᶠ1 Tim. iv. 14–16.—ᵍActs xx. 18–20, 25, 27; 1 Thess. iii. 5; 2 Tim. ii. 24, 25.—ʰRom. xii. 7, 8; 1 Tim. v. 17.

The answer is full and plain.

Q. 28 *Wherein principally doth the authority of the elders of the church consist?*

A. ᵃIn that the rule of the church and the guidance thereof, in things appertaining unto the worship of God, is committed unto them. And, therefore, ᵇwhatever they do as elders in the church, according unto rule, they do it not in the name or authority of the church by which their power is derived unto them, nor as members only of the church by their own consent or covenant, but in the name and authority of Jesus Christ, from whom, by virtue of his law and ordinance, their ministerial office and power are received. So that, ᶜin the exercise of any church-power, by and with the consent of the church, there is an obligation thence proceeding, which ariseth immediately from that authority which they have received of Jesus Christ, which is the spring of all rule and authority in the church.—ᵃActs xx. 28; Heb. xiii. 7, 17; 1 Pet. v. 2; 1 Cor. xii. 28.—ᵇ1 Tim. iii. 5; Col. iv. 17; 2 Cor. x. 4, 8.—ᶜ1 Tim. iv. 11; Titus ii. 15; 1 Pet. v. 2–5.

EXPLICATION. — The answer unto this question explains the power or authority of the elders of the church, from whom they do receive it, and how it is exercised by them; the right stating whereof is of great importance in the whole discipline of the church, and must, therefore, here be farther explained. To this end we may consider, —

First, That all church-power is originally vested in Jesus Christ, the sole head and monarch thereof. God the Father hath committed it unto him, and intrusted him with it for the accomplishment of his work of mediation, Matt. xxviii. 18.

Secondly, That he doth communicate of this authority by way of trust, to be exercised by them in his name, unto persons by him appointed, so much is needful for the ordering and disposing of all things in his churches unto the blessed ends for which he hath instituted and appointed them; for no man can have any power in his church, for any end whatever, but by delegation from him. What is not received from him is mere usurpation. And whoever takes upon himself the exercise of any rule, or authority, or power in the church, not granted unto them by him, or not rightly derived from him, is an oppressor, a "thief and a robber." This necessarily follows upon the absolute investiture of all power in him alone, 1 Cor. xii. 28; Eph. iv. 11, 12.

Thirdly, The means whereby the Lord Christ communicates this power unto men is by his law and constitution, whereby he hath granted, ordained, and appointed, that such and such powers shall be exercised in his church, and that by such and such persons, to be derived unto them in such a way and manner; so that the word of the gospel, or the laws and constitutions of the Lord Christ therein, are the first recipient seat and subject morally of all church-power whatever, Matt. xvi. 19, xviii. 17–20.

Fourthly, The way and means whereby any persons come to a participation of this power regularly, according to the mind of Christ, is by the obedience unto, and due observation of, his laws and commands in them unto whom they are prescribed; as when an office, with the power of it, is constituted and limited by the law of the land, there is no more required to invest any man in that office, or to give him that power, than the due observance of the means and way prescribed in the law to that end. The way, then, whereby the elders of the church do come to participate of the power and authority which Christ hath appointed to be exercised in his church is by their and the church's due observance of the rules and laws given by him for their election and setting apart unto that office, Heb. v. 4, 5; Acts xiv. 23.

Fifthly, On this account they receive their power from Christ himself alone, and that immediately; for the means used for their participation of it are not recipient of the power itself formally, nor do authoritatively collate or confer it, only the laws of Christ are executed in a way of obedience. So that though they are chosen and set apart to their office by the church, yet they are made overseers by the Holy Ghost, Acts xx. 28. Though they have their power *by* the church, yet they have it not *from* the church; nor was that power whereof they are made partakers, as was said, formally resident in the body of the church, before their participation of it, but *really* in Christ himself alone, and *morally* in his word or law. And thence is the rule and guidance of the church committed unto them by Christ, Heb. xiii. 7, 17; 1 Pet. v. 2; 1 Tim. iii. 5.

Sixthly, This authority and power, thus received from Christ, is that which they exert and put forth in all their ministerial administrations, in all which they do as ministers in the house of God, either in his worship or in the rule of the church itself. They exercise that authority of Christ which he hath in his law appointed to be exercised in his church; and from that authority is due order given unto the administration of all the ordinances of worship, and an obligation unto obedience to acts of rule doth thence also ensue; so that they who despise them despise the authority of Christ.

Seventhly, When, as elders, they do or declare any thing in the name of the church, they do not, as such, put forth any authority committed unto them from and by the church, but only declare the consent and determination of the church in the exercise of their own liberty and privilege; but the authority which they act by, and which they put forth, is that which is committed to themselves, as such, by Jesus Christ.

Eighthly, This authority is comprised in the law and constitution of Christ, which themselves exert only *ministerially*; and therefore, when ever they act any thing *authoritatively*, which they are not enabled for or warranted in by the word of the gospel, or do any thing without or contrary unto rule, all such actings, as to any spiritual effect of the gospel, or obligation on the consciences of men, are "ipso facto" null, and are no way ratified in heaven, where all their orderly actings are made valid, — that is, by Christ himself in his word.

Ninthly, The reason, therefore, why the *consent* of the church is required unto the authoritative acting of the elders therein is, not because from thence any authority doth accrue unto them anew, which virtually and radically they had not before, but because by the rule of the gospel this is required to the orderly acting of their power, which without it would be contrary to rule, and therefore ineffectual; as also it must needs be from the nature of the thing itself, for no act can take place in the church without or against its own consent, whilst its obedience is voluntary and of choice.

But if it be asked, "What, then, shall the elders do in case the church refuse to consent unto such acts as are indeed according to rule, and warranted by the institution of Christ?" it is answered, that they are, — 1. Diligently to *instruct* them from the word in their duty, making known the mind of Christ unto them in the matter under consideration; 2. To declare unto them the *danger* of their dissent in obstructing the edification of the body, to the dishonour of the Lord Christ and their own spiritual disadvantage; 3. To *wait patiently* for the concurrence of the grace of God with their ministry in giving light and obedience unto the church; and, 4. In case of the church's continuance in any failure of duty, to seek for advice and *counsel* from the elders and brethren of other churches; — all which particulars might be enlarged, would the nature of our present design and work permit it.

Q. 29 *What is the duty of the church towards their elders, pastors, or teachers?*

A. [a]To have them in reverence and honour for their office and work's sake; [b]to obey them conscientiously in all things wherein they speak unto them in the name of the Lord; [c]to pray earnestly for them, that they may, and to exhort them, if need require, to fulfil the work of the ministry; [d]to communicate unto them of their temporals, for their comfortable subsistence in the world and usefulness unto others; [e]wisely to order things by their direction, so as that they may be amongst them without fear; ᶠto abide with and stand by them in their sufferings for the gospel, and service of Christ among them.—ᵃ1 Thess. v. 12, 13; 1 Tim. v. 17.—ᵇHeb. xiii. 17; 1 Cor. xvi. 16.—ᶜEph. vi. 18, 19; Col. iv. 3; 2 Thess. iii. 1; Col. iv. 17.—ᵈGal. vi. 6; 1 Cor. ix. 14.—ᵉ1 Cor. xvi. 10.—ᶠ2 Tim. i. 16–18, iv. 16.

Q. 30 *Are there any differences in the office or offices of the guides, rulers, elders, or ministers of the church?*

A. The office of them that are teachers is one and the same among them all; but where there are many in the same church, it is the will of Christ that they should be peculiarly assigned unto such especial work, in the discharge of their office-power, as their gifts received from him do peculiarly fit them for and the necessities of the church require.—Rom. xii. 4–8; 1 Cor. xii. 4–6, 8; 1 Pet. iv. 10, v. 2.

EXPLICATION. — The office of them that are to instruct the church in the name and authority of Christ is one and the same, as hath been showed before. And there are many names that are equally accommodated unto all that are partakers of it, as elders, bishops, guides; they are all alike elders, alike bishops, alike guides, — have the one office in common amongst them, and every one the whole entire unto himself. But there are names also given unto them, whereby they are distinguished, not as to office, but as to their work and employment in the discharge of that office: such are "pastors and teachers," Eph. iv. 11, which are placed as distinct persons in their work, partakers of the same office. Now, the foundation of this distinction and difference lies, —

First, In the different gifts that they have received; for although it be required in them all that they have received all those gifts, abilities, and qualifications which are necessary for the work of the ministry, yet as to the degrees of their participation of their gifts, some may more excel in one, others in another: 1 Cor. xii. 4–6, 8, "There are diversities of gifts, but the same Spirit. And there are differences of administrations, but the same Lord. And there are diversities of operations, but it is the same God which worketh all in all. For to one is given by the Spirit the word of wisdom; to another the word of knowledge by the same Spirit," etc. And all these gifts are bestowed upon them to be exercised and laid out for the profit and benefit of the church: Verse 7, "The manifestation of the Spirit is given to every man to profit withal." And therefore every one is in an especial manner to attend unto the exercise and use of that gift wherein he doth excel, or which tends most to the edification of the church, every man being to minister according as he hath received, 1 Pet. iv. 10.

Secondly, It lies in the nature of the work of the ministry in the church, which in general may be referred unto two heads or ends:—

1. The *instruction* of it in the knowledge of God in Christ, and the mysteries of the gospel, that it might grow in grace, wisdom, saving light, and knowledge.

2. The *exhortation* of it to walk answerable unto light received, in holiness and universal obedience. Now, though these several ends of the ministry cannot be divided or separated, yet they may be distinguished, and so carried on distinctly, that in the one, knowledge or light may be firstly and principally intended, so as to lead unto obedience;

in the other, holiness may be firstly designed, as springing from gospel light or knowledge. Hence, therefore, are the elders of the church principally to attend unto that work, or that end of the ministry, which by the Holy Ghost they are most suited unto. And, therefore, the church following the intimations of the Holy Ghost, in communicating his gifts in variety as he pleaseth, and attending to their own edification, may and ought, amongst those whom they choose to the office of elders or ministers, withal design them in particular unto that especial work which they are especially fitted and prepared for; and this, upon their being chosen and set apart, they are accordingly to attend unto: "He that teacheth, on teaching; he that exhorteth, on exhortation," Rom. xii. 7, 8. Their office, then, is the same; but their teaching work and employment, on the grounds mentioned, distinct and different.

Q. 31 *Are there appointed any elders in the church whose office and duty consist in rule and government only?*

A. Elders not called to teach ordinarily or administer the sacraments, but to assist and help in the rule and government of the church, are mentioned in the Scripture.—Rom. xii. 8; 1 Cor. xii. 28; 1 Tim. v. 17.

EXPLICATION. — This office of *ruling elders* in the church is much opposed by some, and in especial by them who have least reason so to do: for, first, they object against them that they are *lay elders*, when those with whom they have to do deny that distinction of the church into the clergy and laity; for although they allow the distribution of it into officers and the multitude of the brethren, yet they maintain that the whole church is God's clergy, his lot, and portion, 1 Pet. v. 3. Again, they affirm them to be elders, and therein not merely of the members of the church, but officers set apart unto their office according to rule, or the appointment of Christ. And if by laity, the people distinct from the officers of the church are to be understood, the very term of a *lay elder* implies a contradiction, as designing one who is and is not a church-officer. Besides, themselves do principally govern the church by such whom they esteem laymen, as not in holy orders, to whom the principal part of its rule, at least in the execution of it, is committed; which renders their objection to this sort of church-officers unreasonable. Others, also, have given advantage by making this office *annual* or *biennial* in them that are chosen unto it; which, though they plead the necessity of their churches for, as not having persons meet for this work and duty who are willing to undertake it constantly during their lives, without such a contribution for their maintenance as they are not able to afford, yet the wisest of them do acknowledge an irregularity in what they do, and wish it remedied. But this hinders not but that such church-officers are indeed designed in the Scripture, and of whom frequent mention is made in the ancient writers, and footsteps also yet remain in most churches of their institution, though woefully corrupted; for besides that some light in this matter may be taken from the church of the Jews, wherein the elders of the people were joined in rule with the priests, both in the sanhedrin and all lesser assemblies, there is in the gospel express mention of persons that were assigned peculiarly for rule and government in the church, as 1 Cor. xii. 28. And it is in vain pretended that those words, "helps, governments," do denote gifts only, seeing the apostle expressly enumerates the persons in office, or officers, which the Lord Christ then used in the foundation and rule of the churches as then planted. He that *ruleth*, also, is distinguished from him that *teacheth* and him that *exhorteth*, Rom. xii. 8; and is prescribed diligence as his principal qualification in the discharge of his duty. And the words of the apostle to this purpose are express: 1 Tim. v. 17, "Let the elders that rule well be counted worthy of double honour, especially those who labour in the word and doctrine." For the words expressly assign two sorts of elders, whereof some only attend unto rule; others, moreover, labour in the word and doctrine. Neither doth that word, as some would have it, "labour in the word," intend any other labour but what is incumbent on all the pastors and teachers of the church as their constant duty. See Rom. xvi. 12; Acts xx. 35; 1 Thess. v. 12. Now, can we suppose that the apostle would affirm them to be worthy of double honour, whom, comparing with others, he notes as remiss and negligent in their work? for it seems that others were more diligent in the discharge of that duty, which was no less theirs, if only one sort of elders be here intended. The Scripture is not wont to commend such persons as worthy of double honour, but rather to propose them as meet for double shame and punishment, Jer. xlviii. 10; 1 Cor. ix. 16. And they are unmindful of their own interest who would have bishops that attend to the rule of the church to be distinctly intended by the elders that rule well, seeing the apostle expressly preferreth before and above them those that attend constantly to the word and doctrine. And besides what is thus expressly spoken concerning the appointment of this sort of elders in the church, their usefulness, in the necessity of their work and employment, is evident; for whereas a constant care in the church that the conversation of all the members of it be such as becometh the gospel, that the name of our Lord Jesus Christ be not evil spoken of, is of great concernment and importance, and the pastors and teachers, being to give up themselves continually unto prayer and the ministry of the word, cannot attend unto the constant and daily oversight thereof, the usefulness of these elders, whose proper and peculiar work it is to have regard unto the holy walking of the church, must needs be manifest unto all. But whereas in most churches there is little or no regard unto the *personal holiness* of the members of them, it is no wonder that no account should be had of them who are ordained by the Lord Christ to look after it and promote it.

The qualification of these elders, with the way of their call and setting apart unto their office, being the same with those of the teaching elders before insisted on, need not be here again repeated. Their authority, also, in the whole rule of the church, is every way the same with that of the other sort of elders; and they are to act in the execution of it with equal respect and regard from the church. Yea, the business of rule being peculiarly committed unto them, and they required to attend thereunto with diligence in an especial manner, the work thereof is principally theirs, as that of labouring in the word and doctrine doth especially belong unto the pastors and teachers of the churches. And this institution is abused when either unmeet persons are called to this office, or those that are called do not attend unto their duty with diligence, or do act only in it by the guidance of the teaching officers, without a sense of their own authority, or due respect from the church.

Q. 32 *Is there no other ordinary office in the church but only that of elders?*
A. Yes, of deacons also.

Q. 33 *What are the deacons of the church?*
A. Approved men chosen by the church to take care for the necessities of the poor belonging thereunto, and other outward occasions of the whole church, by the collection, keeping, and distribution of the alms and other supplies of the church; set apart and commended to the grace of God therein by prayer.—Acts vi. 3, 5, 6; Phil. i. 1; 1 Tim. iii. 8–13.

EXPLICATION. — The office of the deacon, the nature, end, and use of it, the qualifications of the persons to be admitted unto it, the way and manner of their election and setting apart, are all of them plainly expressed in the Scripture: Acts vi. 1–3, 5, 6, "There arose a murmuring of the Grecians against the Hebrews, because their widows were neglected in the daily ministration. Then the twelve called the multitude of the disciples unto them, and said, It is not reason that we should leave the word of God, and serve tables. Wherefore, brethren, look ye out among you seven men of honest report, full of the Holy Ghost and wisdom, whom we may appoint over this business. And the saying pleased the whole multitude: and they chose Stephen," etc., "whom they set before the apostles: and when they had prayed, they laid their hands on them." 1 Tim. iii. 8–13, "Likewise must the deacons be grave, not double-tongued, not given to much wine, not greedy of filthy lucre; holding the mystery of the faith in a pure conscience. And let these also first be proved; then let them use the office of a deacon, being found blameless; the husbands of one wife, ruling their children and their own houses well. For they that have used the office of a deacon well purchase to themselves a good degree, and great boldness in the faith which is in Christ Jesus." These things are thus plain and express in the Scripture. But whereas many have grown weary of the observation of the institutions of the gospel, this office hath for a long time been lost amongst the most of Christians. By some the name is retained, but applied to another work, duty, and employment, than this to which it is peculiarly appropriated in the Scripture. Their proper and original work of taking care for the poor, they say, is provided for by others; and therefore that office being needless, another, unto another purpose, under the same name, is erected. Such are deacons that may read service, preach, and baptize, when they have license thereunto. But this choice, to reject an office of the appointment of Christ, under pretence of provision made for the duties of it another way, and the erecting of one not appointed by him, seems not equal. But whereas it is our duty in all things to have regard to the authority of Christ and his appointments in the gospel, if we claim the privilege of being called after his name, some think that if what he hath appointed may be colourably performed another way without respect unto his institutions, that is far the best; but omitting the practice of other men, the things that concern this office in the church are, as was said, clear in the Scripture.

First, The persons called unto it are to be of

honest report, furnished with the gifts of the Holy Ghost, especially with wisdom, Acts vi. 3, and those other endowments useful in the discharge of their duty mentioned, 1 Tim. iii. 8–13.

Secondly, The way whereby they come to be made partakers of this office is by the choice or *election* of the church, Acts vi. 2, 3, 5, whereupon they are solemnly to be set apart by prayer.

Thirdly, Their work or duty consists in a daily ministration unto the necessities of the poor *saints*, or members of the church, verses 1, 2.

Fourthly, To this end, that they may be enabled so to do, it is ordained that every *first day* [*of the week*] the members of the church do contribute, according as God enables them, of their substance for the supply of the wants of the poor, 1 Cor. xvi. 2; and also occasionally, as necessity shall require, or God move their hearts by his grace.

Fifthly, Hereunto is to be added whatever by the providence of God may be conferred upon the church for its outward advantage, with reference unto the end mentioned, Acts iv. 34, 35.

Sixthly, These supplies of the church being committed to the care and charge of the *deacons*, they are from thence to minister with diligence and wisdom unto the necessities of the poor; that so the needy may be supplied, that there may be none that lack, the rich may contribute of their riches according to the mind of Christ, and in obedience unto his command; that they which minister well in this office "may purchase to themselves a good degree and great boldness in the faith," and that in all the name of our Lord Jesus Christ may be glorified with praise and thanksgiving.

It belongs, therefore, unto persons called unto this office, —

First, To acquaint themselves with the *outward condition* of those that appear to be poor and needy in the church, whether by the addresses of such poor ones, who are bound to make known their wants, occasions, and necessities unto them, or by the information of others, or their own observation.

Secondly, To acquaint the elders and the church, as occasion requireth, with the necessities of the poor under their care, that those who are able may be stirred up by the elders to a free supply and contribution.

Thirdly, To dispose of what they are intrusted with *faithfully*, cheerfully, tenderly, without partiality or preferring one before another, for any outward respect whatever.

Fourthly, To keep and give an account unto the church, when called for, of what they have received, and how they have disposed of it; that so they may be known to have well discharged their office, — that is, with care, wisdom, and tenderness, — whereby they procure to themselves a good degree, with boldness in the faith, and the church is encouraged to intrust them farther with this sacrifice of their alms, which is so acceptable unto God.

Q. 34 *Wherein consists the general duty of the whole church, and every member thereof, in their proper station and condition?*

A. In performing, doing, and keeping inviolate all the commands and institutions of Jesus Christ, walking unblamably and fruitfully in the world, holding forth the word of truth, and glorifying the Lord Christ in and by the profession of his name, and keeping his testimony unto the end.—Matt. xxviii. 20; Acts ii. 42; Phil. ii. 15, 16, iv. 8, 9; 1 Thess.

iii. 8; 1 Pet. iv. 10–14; 1 Tim. iii. 15; Heb. x. 23.

EXPLICATION. — Besides the general duties of Christianity incumbent on all believers or disciples of Christ, as such, there are sundry especial duties required of them as gathered into church-societies, upon the account of an especial trust committed unto them in that state and condition; for, —

First, The church being appointed as the *seat* and subject of all the institutions of Christ and ordinances of Gospel worship, it is its duty, — that is, of the whole body, and every member in his proper place, — to use all care, watchfulness, and diligence that all the commands of Christ be kept inviolate, and all his institutions observed according to his mind and will. Thus, those "added to the church," Acts ii. 42, together with the whole church, "continued stedfastly" (which argues care, circumspection, and diligence) "in the apostles' doctrine and fellowship, and breaking of bread, and in prayers;" which principal duties are enumerated to express their respect towards all. This is their "standing fast in the Lord," which was a matter of such joy to the apostle when he found it in the Thessalonians, 1 Epist. iii. 8, "For now we live, if ye stand fast in the Lord;" — that order and steadfastness which he rejoiced over in the Colossians, chap ii. 5 "For though I be absent in the flesh, yet I am with you in the spirit, joying and beholding your order, and the steadfastness of your faith in Christ." And where this duty is despised, men contenting themselves with what is done by others, there is a great neglect of that faithfulness in obedience which the church owes unto Jesus Christ.

Secondly, The *glory* of the Lord Christ, and the doctrine of the gospel, to be manifested in and by the power of a holy, exemplary conversation, is committed unto the church and all the members of it. This is one end wherefore the Lord Christ calls them out of the world, separates them to be a peculiar people unto himself, brings them forth unto a visible profession, and puts his name upon them, — namely, that in their walking and conversation he may show forth the holiness of his doctrine, and power of his Spirit, grace, and example, to effect in them all holiness, godliness, righteousness, and honesty in the world. Hence are they earnestly exhorted unto these things: Phil. iv. 8, "Brethren, whatsoever things are true, whatsoever things are honest, whatsoever things are just, whatsoever things are pure, whatsoever things are lovely, whatsoever things are of good report; if there be any virtue, and if there be any praise, think on these things;" and that to this end, that the doctrine of the gospel may be adorned, and Christ glorified in all things, Titus ii. 10. And those who fail herein are said to be "the enemies of the cross of Christ," Phil. iii. 18, as hindering the progress of the doctrine thereof, by rendering it undesirable in their conversation. This also, therefore, even the duty of universal holiness, with an especial regard unto the honour of Christ and the gospel, which they are called and designed to testify and express in the world, is incumbent on the church, and every member of it, namely, as the apostle speaks, "that they may be blameless and harmless, the sons of God, without rebuke, in the midst of a crooked and perverse nation," among whom they are to "shine as lights in the world," Phil. ii. 15.

Thirdly, The care of *declaring* and manifesting the truth is also committed unto them. Christ hath made the church to be the "pillar and ground of the truth," 1 Tim. iii. 15; where the truth of the gospel is to be firmly seated, founded, fixed, established, and then lifted up in the ways of Christ's appointment, to be seen, discerned, and known by others. And as this is done principally in the preaching of the gospel by the elders of the church, and in their "contending for the faith once delivered unto the saints," Jude 3, so it is also the duty of the whole church to "hold forth the word of life," Phil. ii. 16, by ministering of "the gifts that every man hath received," 1 Pet. iv. 10, in the way of Christ's appointment. In these and the like instances doth our Lord Jesus Christ require of his church that they express in the world their subjection unto him and his authority; and that they abide therein unto the end against all opposition whatever.

The sinful neglect of churches in the discharge of their duty herein was one great means of that apostasy from the rule of the gospel which they generally of old fell into. When the members of them began to think that they had no advantage by their state and condition, but only the outward participation of some ordinances of worship, and no duty incumbent on them but only to attend and follow the motions and actings of their guides, the whole societies quickly became corrupt, and fit to be disposed of according to the carnal interest of those that had by their neglect and sin gotten dominion over them. And at all times, as the people were negligent in their duty, the *leaders* of them were apt to usurp undue authority. When the one sort will not do that which they ought, the other are ready to take upon them what they ought not. It is a circumspect performance of duty on all hands alone that will keep all sorts of persons in the church within those bounds and limits, and up to those rights and privileges, which Christ hath allotted and granted unto them. And herein alone doth the order, honour, and beauty of the church consist. Church-members, therefore, are to search and inquire after the particular duties which, as such, are incumbent on them; as also to consider what influence their special state and condition, as they are church-members, ought to have into all the duties of their obedience as they are Christians: for this privilege is granted unto them for their edification; that is, their furtherance in their whole course of walking before God. And if this be neglected, — if they content themselves with a name to live in this or that church, to partake of the ordinances that are stated and solemnly administered only, — that which would have been to their advantage may prove to be a snare and temptation unto them. What these especial duties are, in the particular instances of them, is of too large a consideration here to be insisted on. Besides, it is the great duty of the guides of the church to be inculcating of them into the minds of those committed to their charge; for the church's due performance of its duty is their honour, crown, and reward.

Q. 35 *Whence do you reckon prayer, which is a part of moral and natural worship, among the institutions of Christ in his church?*

A. On many accounts; as, — [a]because the Lord Christ hath commanded his church to attend unto the worship of God therein; [b]because he bestows on the ministers of the church gifts and ability of prayer for the benefit and edification thereof; [c]he hath appointed that all his other ordinances should be administered with prayer, whereby it becomes a part of them; ᵈbecause himself ministers in the holy place, as the great high priest of his church, to present their prayers unto God at the throne of grace; ᵉbecause in all the prayers of the church there is an especial regard had unto himself and the whole work of his mediation.—ᵃLuke xviii. 1, xxi. 36; Rom. xii. 12; 1 Tim. ii. 1, 2.—ᵇEph. iv. 8, 12, 13; Rom. viii. 15, 16; Gal. iv. 6.—ᶜActs ii. 42; 1 Tim. iv. 5.—ᵈRev. viii. 3, 4; Heb. iv. 14–16, vi. 20, x. 19–22.—ᵉJohn xiv. 13, John xv. 16, xvi. 23, 26; Eph. iii. 14, 15.

Q. 36 *May not the church, in the solemn worship of God, and celebration of the ordinances of the gospel, make use of and content itself in the use of forms of prayer in an unknown tongue composed by others, and prescribed unto them?*

A. So to do would be ᵃcontrary to one principal end of prayer itself, which is, that believers may therein apply themselves to the throne of grace for spiritual supplies according to the present condition, wants, and exigencies of their souls; ᵇto the main end that the Lord Jesus Christ aimed at in supplying men with gifts for the discharge of the work of the ministry, tending to render the promise of sending the Holy Ghost, which is the immediate cause of the church's preservation and continuance, needless and useless. Moreover, ᶜit will render the discharge of the duty of ministers unto several precepts and exhortations of the gospel, for the use, stirring up, and exercise of their gifts, impossible; and ᵈthereby hinder the edification of the church, the great end of all ordinances and institutions.—ᵃRom. viii. 26; Phil. iv. 6; Heb. iv. 16; 1 Pet. iv. 7.—ᵇEph. iv. 8, 12, 13.—ᶜ1 Tim. iv. 14; 2 Tim. i. 6, 7; Col. iv. 17; Matt. xxv. 14–17.—ᵈ1 Cor.

xii. 7.

Q. 37 *Is the constant work of preaching the gospel by the elders of the church necessary?*

A. It is so, both on the part of the elders or ministers themselves, of whom that duty is strictly required, and who principally therein labour and watch for the good of the flock, and on the part of the church, for the furtherance of their faith and obedience, by instruction, reproof, exhortation, and consolation.—Matt. xxiv. 45–51; Rom. xii. 7, 8; 1 Cor. ix. 17, 18; Eph. iv. 11–13; 1 Tim. iv. 15, 16, v. 17; 2 Tim. ii. 24, 25, iii. 14–17, iv. 2.

Q. 38 *Who are the principal subjects of baptism?*

A. Professing believers, if not baptized in their infancy, and their infant seed.—Matt. xxviii. 19; Acts ii. 38, 39, xvi. 33; 1 Cor. i. 16, vii. 14; Col. ii. 12–14, with Gen. xvii. 10–12.

Q. 39 *Where and to whom is the ordinance of the Lord's supper to be administered?*

A. In the church, or assembly of the congregation, to all the members of it, rightly prepared and duly assembled, or to such of them as are so assembled.—1 Cor. xi. 20–22, 28, 29, 33; Acts ii. 46.

Q. 40 *How often is that ordinance to be administered?*

A. Every first day of the week, or at least as often as opportunity and conveniency may be obtained.—1 Cor. xi. 26; Acts xx. 7.

Q. 41 *What is the discipline of the church?*

A. It consists in the due exercise of that authority and power which the Lord Christ, in and by his word, hath granted unto the church, for its continuance, increase, and preservation in purity, order, and holiness, according to his appointment.—Matt. xvi. 19; Rom. xii. 8; 2 Cor. x. 4–6; Rev. ii. 2, 20.

EXPLICATION. — Sundry things are to be considered about this discipline of the church; as, —

First, The *foundation* of it, which is a grant of power and authority made unto it by Jesus Christ as mediator, head, king, and lawgiver of his church; for all discipline being an act of power, and this being exercised in and about things internal and spiritual, no men can of themselves, or by grant of any others, have any right or authority to or in the exercise thereof. Whoever hath any interest herein or right hereunto, it must be granted unto him from above by Jesus Christ, and that as mediator and head of his church; for as all church-power is in an especial manner, by the authority and grant of the Father, vested in him alone, Matt. xxviii. 18, Eph. i. 20–23, so the *nature* of it, which is spiritual, the *objects* of it, which are the consciences and gospel privileges of believers, with the *ends* of it, — namely, the glory of God in Christ, with the spiritual and eternal good of the souls of men, — do all manifest that it can have no other right nor foundation. This in the first place is to be fixed, that no authority can be exercised in the church but what is derived from Jesus Christ, as was spoken before.

Secondly, The *means* whereby the Lord Christ doth communicate this power and authority unto his church in his word or his law and constitution concerning it in the gospel; so that it is exactly limited and bounded thereby. And no power or authority can be exercised in the church but what is granted and conveyed unto it by the word, seeing that Christ communicates no power or authority any other ways. Whatever of that nature is beside it or beyond it is mere usurpation, and null in its exercise. Herein is the commission of the guides and rulers of the church expressed, which they are not to exceed in any thing. Herein are bounds and limits fixed to the actings of the whole church, and of every part and member of it.

Thirdly, This power or authority, thus granted and conveyed by Jesus Christ, is to be exercised, as to the *manner* of the administration of discipline, with skill and diligence, Rom. xii. 8; 1 Cor. xii. And the skill required hereunto is a gift, or an ability of mind, bestowed by the Holy Ghost upon men, to put in execution the laws of Christ for the government of the church in the way and order by him appointed, or a spiritual wisdom, whereby men know how to behave themselves in the house of God in their several places, for its due edification in faith and love, 1 Tim. iii. 15. And this ability of mind to make a due application of the laws of the gospel unto persons, times, and actions, with their circumstances, is such a gift of the Holy Ghost as whereof there are several degrees, answering to the distinct duties that are incumbent on the rulers of the church on the one hand, and the members on the other. And where this skill and wisdom is wanting, there it is impossible that the discipline of the church should be preserved or carried on. Hereunto also diligence and watchfulness are to be added, without which ability and power will never obtain their proper end in a due manner, Rom. xii. 6–8.

Fourthly, The *end* of this discipline is the continuance, increase, and preservation of the church, according to the rule of its first institution, 1 Cor. v. 7. This power hath Christ given his church for its conservation, without which it must necessarily decay and come to nothing. Nor is it to be imagined that where any church is called and gathered according to the mind of Christ, he hath left it destitute of power and authority to preserve itself in that state and order which he hath appointed unto it. And that which was one principal cause of the decays of the Asian churches was the neglect of this discipline, the power and privilege whereof the Lord had left unto them and intrusted them withal, for their own preservation in order, purity, and holiness. And, therefore, for the neglect thereof they were greatly blamed by him, Rev. ii. 14, 15, 20, iii. 1, 2; as is also the church of Corinth by the apostle, 1 Cor. v. 2; as they are commended who attended unto the diligent exercise of it, Rev. ii. 2, iii. 9. The disuse, also, of it hath been the occasion of all the defilements, abominations, and confusions that have spread themselves over many churches in the world.

Q. 42 *Unto whom is the power and administration of this discipline committed by Jesus Christ?*

A. As to the authority to be exerted in it, in the things wherein the whole church is concerned, unto the elders; as unto trial, judgment, and consent in and unto its exercise, unto the whole brotherhood; as unto love, care, and watchfulness in private and particular cases, to every member of the church.—Matt. xxiv. 45; Eph. iv. 11, 12; Acts xx. 28; 1 Tim. iii. 5, v. 17; Heb. xiii. 7, 17; 1 Pet. v. 2; 1 Thess. v. 12; Gal. vi. 1, 2; 1 Cor. iv. 14, v. 2, 4, 5; 2 Cor. ii. 6–8; 2 Tim. iv. 2.

EXPLICATION. — It hath been showed that this power is granted unto the church by virtue of the *law* and constitution of Christ. Now, this law assigns the means and way whereby any persons do obtain an interest therein, and makes the just allotments to all concerned in it. What this law, constitution, or word of Christ assigns unto any, as such, that they are the first seat and subject of, by what way or means soever they come to be intrusted therein. Thus, that power or authority which is given unto the elders of the church doth not first formally reside in the body of the church unorganized or distinct from them, though they are called unto their office by their suffrage and choice; but they are themselves, as such, the first subject of office-power, for so is the will of the Lord Christ. Nor is the interest of the whole church in this power of discipline, whatever it be, given unto it by the elders, but is immediately granted unto it by the will and law of the Lord Jesus.

First, In this way and manner the authority above described is given in the first place, as such, unto the *elders* of the church. This authority was before explained, in answer unto the 28th question; as also was the way whereby they receive it. And it is that power of office whereby they are enabled for the discharge of their whole duty, in the teaching and ruling of the church, called the "power of the keys," from Matt. xvi. 19; which expression being metaphorical, and in general liable unto many interpretations, is to be understood according to the declaration made of it in those particular instances wherein it is expressed. Nor is it a twofold power or authority that the elders of the church have committed unto them, — one to teach and another to rule, commonly called the power of order and of jurisdiction; but it is one power of office, the duties whereof are of several kinds, referred unto the two general heads, first of teaching, by preaching the word and celebration of the sacraments, and secondly, of rule or government. By virtue hereof are they made rulers over the house of God, Matt. xxiv. 45; stewards in his house, 1 Cor. iv. 1; overseers of the church, Acts xx. 28, 1 Pet. v. 2; guides unto the church, Heb. xiii. 7, 17. Not that they have a supreme or *autocratorical* power committed unto them, to enable them to do what seems right and good in their own eyes, seeing they are expressly bound up unto the terms of their commission, Matt. xxviii. 19, 20, *to teach men to do and observe all and only what Christ hath commanded*; nor have they by virtue of it any dominion in or over the church, — that is, the laws, rules, or privileges of it, — or the consciences of the disciples of Christ, to alter, change, add, diminish, or bind by their own authority, 1 Pet. v. 3, Mark x. 42–44. But it is a power merely *ministerial*, in whose exercise they are unto the Lord Christ accountable servants, Heb. xiii. 17, Matt. xxiv. 45, and servants of the church for Jesus' sake, 2 Cor. iv. 5. This authority, in the discipline of the church they exert and put forth by virtue of their office, and not either as declaring of the power of the church itself, or acting what is delegated unto them thereby, but as ministerially exercising the authority of Christ committed unto themselves.

Secondly, The body of the church, or the multitude of the brethren (women being excepted by especial prohibition, 1 Cor. xiv. 34, 35, 1 Tim. ii. 11, 12), is, by the law and constitution of Christ in the gospel, interested in the administration of this power of discipline in the church, so far as, —

1. To consider, try, and make a judgment in and about all persons, things, and causes, in reference whereunto it is to be exercised. Thus, the

brethren at Jerusalem joined in the consideration of the observation of Mosaical ceremonies with the apostles and elders, Acts xv. 23; and the multitude of them to whom letters were sent about it likewise did the same, verses 30–32; and this they thought it their duty and concernment to do, chap. xxi. 22. And they are blamed who applied not themselves unto this duty, 1 Cor. v. 2–6. Thence are the epistles of Paul to the churches to instruct them in their duties and privileges in Christ, and how they ought to behave themselves in the ordering of all things amongst them according to his mind. And these are directed unto the churches themselves, either jointly with their elders, or distinctly from them, Phil. i. 1. And the whole preservation of church-order is, on the account of this duty, recommended unto them. Neither can what they do in compliance with their guides and rulers be any part of their obedience unto the Lord Christ, unless they make previously thereunto a rational consideration and judgment, by the rule, of what is to be done. Neither is the church of Christ to be ruled without its knowledge or against its will; nor in any thing is blind obedience acceptable to God.

2. The brethren of the church are intrusted with the privilege of giving and testifying their consent unto all acts of church-power, which, though it belong not formally unto the authority of them, is necessary unto their validity and efficacy; and that so far forth as that they are said to do and act what is done and effected thereby, 1 Cor. v. 4, 5, 13; 2 Cor. ii. 6–8. And they who have this privilege of consent, which hath so great an influence into the action and validity of it, have also the liberty of dissent, when any thing is proposed to be done, the warrant whereof from the word and the rule of

its performance are not evident unto them.

Q. 43 *Wherein doth the exercise of the authority for discipline committed unto the elders of the church consist?*

A. ᵃIn personal private admonition of any member or members of the church, in case of sin, error, or any miscarriage known unto themselves; ᵇin public admonition in case of offences persisted in, and brought orderly to the knowledge and consideration of the church; ᶜin the ejection of obstinate offenders from the society and communion of the church; ᵈin exhorting, comforting, and restoring to the enjoyment and exercise of church-privileges such as are recovered from the error of their ways; — all according to the laws, rules, and directions of the gospel.—ᵃMatt. xviii. 15; 1 Thess. v. 14; 1 Cor. iv. 14; Titus i. 13, , ii. 15; 2 Tim. iv. 2.—ᵇ1 Tim. v. 19, 20; Matt. xviii. 16, 17.—ᶜTitus iii. 10; 1 Tim. i. 20; Matt. xviii. 17; 1 Cor. v. 5; Gal. v. 12.—ᵈ2 Cor. ii. 7, 8; Gal. vi. 1; 2 Thess. iii. 15.

Q. 44 *May the church cast any person out of its communion without previous admonition?*

A. It may in some cases, where the offence is notorious and the scandal grievous, so that nothing be done against other general rules.—1 Cor. v.

Q. 45 *Wherein doth the liberty and duty of the whole brotherhood in the exercise of discipline in the church in particular consist?*

A. ᵃIn a meek consideration of the condition and temptations of offenders, with the nature of their offences, when orderly proposed unto the church; ᵇin judging with the elders, according to rule, what, in all cases of offence, is necessary to be done for the good of the offenders themselves, and for the edification and vindication of the whole church, ᶜin their consent unto, and concurrence in, the admonition, ejection, pardoning, and restoring of offenders, as the matter shall require.—ᵃGal. vi. 1, 2;—ᵇ1 Cor. v. 2, 4, 5, 12, vi. 2;—ᶜ2 Cor. ii. 6–8.

Q. 46 *What is the duty of private members in reference unto the discipline appointed by Christ in his church?*

A. It is their duty, in their mutual watch over one another, to exhort each other unto holiness and perseverance; and if they observe any thing in the ways and walkings of any of their fellow-members not according unto the rule and duty of their profession, which, therefore, gives them offence, to admonish them thereof in private, with love, meekness, and wisdom; and in case they prevail not unto their amendment, to take the assistance of some other brethren in the same work; and if they fail in success therein also, to report the matter, by the elders' direction, unto the whole church.—Matt. xviii. 16–18; 1 Thess. v. 14.

EXPLICATION. — In these questions an inquiry is made after the exercise of discipline in the church, — as to that part of it which belongs unto the reproof and correction of miscarriages, according to the distribution of right, power, and privilege before explained.

The first act hereof consists in *private admonition*; for so hath our Lord ordained, that in case any brother or member of the church do in any thing walk disorderly, and not according to the rule of the gospel, he or they unto whom it is observed, and who are thereby offended, may and ought to admonish the person or persons so offending of their miscarriages and offence; concerning which is to be observed, —

First, What is previously required thereunto; and that is, —

1. That in all the members of the church there ought to be "love without dissimulation." They are to "be kindly affectioned one to another with brotherly love," Rom. xii. 9, 10; which as they are taught of God, so they are greatly exhorted thereunto, Heb. xiii. 1. This love is the bond of perfection, the most excellent way and means of preserving church-order, and furthering the edification thereof, 1 Cor. xiii., without which, well seated and confirmed in the hearts and minds of church-members, no duty of their relation can ever be performed in a due manner.

2. This love is to exert and put forth itself in tender care and watchfulness for the good of each other; which are to work by mutual exhortations, informations, instructions, according as opportunities do offer themselves, or as the necessities of any do seem to require, Heb. iii. 13, x. 24.

Secondly, This duty of admonishing offenders privately and personally is common to the elders with all the members of the church; neither doth it belong properly unto the elders as such, but as brethren of the same society. And yet, by virtue of their office, the elders are enabled to do it with more authority morally, though office-power properly be not exercised therein. By virtue, also, of their constant general watch over the whole flock in the discharge of their office, they are enabled to take notice of and discern miscarriages in any of the members sooner than others: but as to the exercise of the discipline of the church in this matter, this duty is equally incumbent on every member of it, according as the obligation on them to watch over one another, and to exercise especial love towards each other, is equal; whence it is distinguished from that private pastoral admonition, which is an act of the teaching office and power, not directly belonging unto the rule or government inquired after. But this admonition is an effect of love; and when it proceedeth not from thence it is irregular, Matt. xviii. 16–18; Rom. xv. 14.

Thirdly, This duty is so incumbent on every member of the church, that in case of the neglect thereof, he both sinneth against the institution of Christ and makes himself partaker of the sin of the party offending, and is also guilty of his danger and ruin thereby, with all that disadvantage which will accrue to the church by any of the members of it continuing in sin against the rule of the gospel. They have not only liberty thus to admonish one another, but it is their express and indispensable duty so to do; the neglect whereof is interpreted by God to be "hatred of our brother," such as wherewith the love of God is inconsistent, Lev. xix. 17; 1 John iii. 15, iv. 20.

Fourthly, Although this duty be personally incumbent on every individual member of the church, yet this hinders not but if the sin of an offender be known to more than one at the same time, and they jointly take offence thereat, they may together in the first instance admonish him, which yet still is but the first and private admonition; which is otherwise when others are called into assistance who are not themselves acquainted with the offence, but only by information, and join in it, not upon the account of their own being offended, but of being desired according unto rule to give assistance to them that are so.

Fifthly, The way and manner of the discharge of this duty is, that it be done with prudence, tenderness, and due regard unto all circumstances; whence the apostle supposeth a spiritual ability to be necessary for this work: Rom. xv. 14, "Ye also are full of goodness, filled with all knowledge, able also to admonish one another." Especially four things are to be diligently heeded: —

1. That the whole duty be so managed that the person *offending* may be convinced that it is done out of love to him and affectionate, conscientious care over him, that he may take no occasion thereby for the exasperation of his own spirit.

2. That the persons admonishing others of their offence do make it appear that what they do is in obedience unto an institution of Christ, and therein to preserve their own souls from sin, as well as to benefit the offenders.

3. That the admonition be grounded on a rule; which alone gives it authority and efficacy.

4. That there be a readiness manifested by them to receive satisfaction, — either (1.) in case that, upon trial, it appeareth the information they have had of the miscarriage whence the offence arose was undue or not well grounded; or, (2.) of acknowledgement and repentance.

Sixthly, The ends of this ordinance and institution of Christ are, —

1. To keep up love without dissimulation among all the members of the church; for if offences should abide unremoved, love, which is the bond of perfection, would not long continue in sincerity, which tends to the dissolution of the whole society.

2. To gain the offender, by delivering him from the guilt of sin, that he may not lie under it, and procure the wrath of God against himself, Lev. xix. 17.

3. To preserve his person from dishonour and disreputation, and thereby to keep up his usefulness in the church. To this end hath our Lord appointed this discharge of this duty in private, that the failings of men may not be unnecessarily divulged, and themselves thereby exposed unto temptation.

4. To preserve the church from that scandal that might befall it by the hasty opening of all the real or supposed failings of its members. And, —

5. To prevent its trouble in the public hearing of things that may be otherwise healed and removed.

Seventhly, In case these ends are obtained, either by the supposed offending persons *clearing of themselves* and manifesting themselves innocent of the crimes charged on them, as Josh. xxii. 21–29, 2 Cor. vii. 11, or by their *acknowledgement*, repentance, and amendment, then this part of the discipline of the church hath, through the grace of Christ, obtained its appointed effect.

Eighthly, In case the persons offending be not humbled nor reformed, nor do give satisfaction unto them by whom they are admonished, then hath our Lord ordained a second degree of this private exercise of discipline:— that the persons who, being offended, have discharged the foregoing duty themselves according unto rule, shall take unto them others, — two or three, as the occasion may seem to require, — to join with them in the same work and duty, to be performed in the same manner, for the same ends, with that before described, Matt. xviii. 15–17. And it is the duty of these persons so called in for assistance, —

1. To judge of the crime, fault, or offence reported to them, and not to proceed unless they find it to consist in something expressly contrary to the

rule of the gospel, and attested in such a manner and with such evidence as their mutual love doth require in them with respect unto their brethren. And they are to judge of the testimony that is given concerning the truth of the offence communicated unto them, that they may not seem either lightly to take up a report against their brother or to discredit the testimony of others.

2. In case they find the offence pretended not to be a real offence, indeed contrary to the rule of the gospel, or that it is not aright grounded as to the evidence of it, but taken up upon prejudice or an over-easy credulity, contrary to the law of that love which is required amongst church-members, described 1 Cor. xiii., and commanded as the great means of the edification of the church and preservation of its union, then to convince the brother offended of his mistake, and with him to satisfy the person pretended to be the offender, that no breach or schism may happen among the members of the same body.

3. Being satisfied of the crime and testimony, they are to associate themselves with the offended brother in the same work and duty that he himself had before discharged towards the offender.

Ninthly, Because there is no determination how often these private admonitions are to be used in case of offence, it is evident from the nature of the thing itself that they are to be reiterated, first the one and then the other, whilst there is any ground of hope that the ends of them may be obtained, through the blessing of Christ, — the brother gained, and the offence taken away. Neither of these, then, is to be deserted or laid aside on the first or second attempt, as though it were performed only to make way for somewhat farther;

but it is to be waited on with prayer and patience, as an ordinance of Christ appointed for attaining the end aimed at.

Tenthly, In case there be not the success aimed at obtained in these several degrees of private admonition, it is then the will of our Lord Jesus Christ that the matter be reported unto the church, that the offended may be publicly admonished thereby and brought to repentance; wherein is to be observed, —

1. That the persons who have endeavoured in vain to reclaim their offending brother by private admonition are to acquaint the elders of the church with the case and crime, as also what they have done according to rule for the rectifying of it; who, upon that information, are obliged to communicate the knowledge of the whole matter to the church. This is to be done by the elders, as to whom the preservation of order in the church and the rule of its proceedings do belong, as we have showed before.

2. The report made to the church by the elders is to be, — (1.) Of the *crime*, guilt, or offence; (2.) Of the *testimony* given unto the truth of it; (3.) Of the *means* used to bring the offender to acknowledgment and repentance; (4.) Of his *deportment* under the private previous admonitions, either as to his rejecting of them, or as to any satisfaction tendered; all in order, love, meekness, and tenderness.

3. Things being proposed unto the church, and the offender heard upon the whole of the offence and former proceeding, the whole church or multitude of the brethren are, with the elders, to consider the nature of the offence, with the condition and temptation of the offender, with such a spirit of meekness as our Lord Jesus Christ, in his own

person, set them an example of in his dealing with sinners, and which is required in them as his disciples, Gal. vi. 1, 2; 2 Cor. ii. 8.

4. The elders and brethren are to judge of the offence and the carriage of the offender according to rule; and if the offence be evident and persisted in, then, —

5. The offender is to be *publicly admonished* by the elders, with the consent and concurrence of the church, 1 Thess. v. 14; 1 Tim. v. 20; Matt. xviii. 17. And this admonition consists of five parts:— (1.) A declaration of the *crime* or offence, as it is evidenced unto the church. (2.) A conviction of the *evil* of it, from the rule or rules transgressed against. (3.) A declaration of the *authority* and duty of the church in such cases. (4.) A rebuke of the offender in the name of Christ, answering the nature and circumstances of the offence. (5.) An exhortation unto *humiliation*, and repentance, and acknowledgment.

Eleventhly, In case the offender despise this admonition of the church, and come not upon it unto repentance, it is the will and appointment of our Lord Jesus Christ that he be *cut off* from all the privileges of the church, and cast out from the society thereof, or be excommunicated; wherein consists the last act of the discipline of the church for the correction of offenders. And herein may be considered, —

1. The *nature* of it, that it is an *authoritative act*, and so principally belongs unto the elders of the church, who therein exert the power that they have received from the Lord Christ, by and with the consent of the church, according to his appointment, Matt. xvi. 19, xviii. 18; John xx. 23; 1 Cor. v. 4, 5; Titus iii. 10; 1 Tim. i. 20; 2 Cor. ii. 6.

And both these, the authority of the eldership and the consent of the brethren, are necessary to the validity of the sentence, and that according to the appointment of Christ, and the practice of the first churches.

2. The *effect* of it, which is the cutting off or casting out of the person offending from the communion of the church, in the privileges of the gospel, as consequently from that of all the visible churches of Christ in the earth, by virtue of their communion one with another; whereby he is left unto the visible kingdom of Satan in the world.—Matt. xviii. 17; 1 Cor. v. 2, 5, 13; 1 Tim. i. 20; Titus iii. 10; Gal. v. 12.

3. The *ends* of it, which are, —

(1.) The *gaining* of the party offending, by bringing him to repentance, humiliation, and acknowledgment of his offence, 2 Cor. ii. 6, 7, xiii. 10.

(2.) The *warning* of others not to do so presumptuously.

(3.) The *preserving* of the church in its purity and order, 1 Cor. v. 6, 7; all to the glory of Jesus Christ.

4. The *causes* of it, or the grounds and reasons on which the church may proceed unto sentence against any offending persons. Now, these are no other but such as they judge, according to the gospel, that the Lord Christ will proceed upon in his final judgment at the last day; for the church judgeth in the name and authority of Christ, and are to exclude none from its communion but those whom they find by the rule that he himself excludes from his kingdom; and so that which they bind on earth is bound by him in heaven, Matt. xviii. 18. And their sentence herein is to be declared, as the declaration of the sentence which the Head of the

church and Judge of all will pronounce at the last day; only with this difference, that it is also made known that this sentence of theirs is not final or decretory, but in order to the prevention of that which will be so unless the evil be repented of. Now, although the particular evils, sins, or offences that may render a person obnoxious unto this censure and sentence are not to be enumerated, by reason of the variety of circumstances, which change the nature of actions, yet they may in general be referred unto these heads:—

(1.) *Moral evils*, contrary to the light of nature and express commands or prohibitions of the moral law, direct rules of the gospel, or of evil report in the world amongst men walking according to the rule and light of reason. And, in cases of this nature, the church may proceed unto the sentence whereof we speak without previous admonition, in case the matter of fact be notorious, publicly and unquestionably known to be true, and no general rule (which is not to be impeached by particular instances) lie against their procedure, 1 Cor. v. 3–5; 2 Tim. iii. 2–5.

(2.) Offences against that *mutual love* which is the bond of perfection in the church, if pertinaciously persisted in, Matt. xviii. 16, 17.

(3.) *False doctrines* against the fundamentals in faith or worship, especially if maintained with contention, to the trouble and disturbance of the peace of the church, Gal. v. 12; Titus iii. 9–11; 1 Tim. vi. 3–5; Rev. ii. 14, 15.

(4.) Blasphemy or evil speaking of the ways and worship of God in the church, especially if joined with an intention to hinder the prosperity of the church or to expose it to persecution, 1 Tim. i. 20.

(5.) Desertion, or total causeless relinquishment of the society and communion of the church; for such are self-condemned, having broken and renounced the covenant of God, that they made at their entrance into the church, Heb. x. 25–31.

5. The *time* or season of the putting forth the authority of Christ in the church for this censure is to be considered, and that is ordinarily after the admonition before described, and that with due waiting, to be regulated by a consideration of times, persons, temptations, and other circumstances; for, —

(1.) The church in proceeding to this sentence is to express the patience and long-suffering of Christ towards offenders, and not to put it forth without conviction of a present resolved impenitency.

(2.) The event and effect of the preceding ordinance of admonition is to be expected; which though not at present evident, yet, like the word itself in the preaching of it, may be blessed to a good issue after many days.

6. The person offending thus cut off, or cast out from the present actual communion of the church, is still to be looked on and accounted as a brother, because of the nature of the ordinance which is intended for his amendment and recovery, — 2 Thess. iii. 15, "Count him not as an enemy, but admonish him as a brother," — unless he manifests his final impenitency by blasphemy and persecution: 1 Tim. i. 20, "Whom I have declared unto Satan, that they may learn not to blaspheme."

7. The church is, therefore, still to perform the duties of love and care towards such persons, —

(1.) In *praying* for them, that they "may be converted from the error of their way," James v. 19, 20. 1 John v. 16, "If any man see his brother sin a sin which is not unto death, he shall ask, and he shall give him life for them that sin not unto death."

(2.) In *withdrawing* from them even as to ordinary converse, for their conviction of their state and condition, 1 Cor. v. 11, "With such an one no not to eat;" 2 Thess. iii. 14.

(3.) In *admonishing* of him: 2 Thess. iii. 15, "Admonish him as a brother:" which may be done, — [1.] *Occasionally*, by any member of the church; [2.] *On set purpose*, by the consent and appointment of the whole church: which admonition is to contain, — 1st, A *pressing of his sin* from the rule on the conscience of the offender; 2dly, A *declaration* of the nature of the censure and punishment which he lieth under; 3dly, A *manifestation* of the danger of his impenitency, in his being either hardened by the deceitfulness of sin or exposed unto new temptations of Satan.

8. In case the Lord Jesus be pleased to give a blessed effect unto this ordinance, in the repentance of the person cut off and cast out of the church, he is, —

(1.) To be *forgiven* both by those who in an especial manner were offended at him and by him, and by the whole church, Matt. xviii. 18; 2 Cor. ii. 7.

(2.) To be *comforted* under his sorrow, 2 Cor. ii. 7, and that by, — [1.] The *application of the promises* of the gospel unto his conscience; [2.] A *declaration of the readiness* of the church to receive him again into their love and communion.

(3.) *Restored*, — [1.] By a *confirmation* or testification of the love of the church unto him, 2 Cor. ii. 8; [2.] A *re-admission* unto the exercise and enjoyment of his former privileges in the fellowship of the church; all with a spirit of meekness, Gal. vi. 1.

Q. 47 *The preservation of the church in purity, order, and holiness, being provided for, by what way is it to be continued and increased?*

A. The way appointed thereunto is by adding such as, being effectually called unto the obedience of faith, shall voluntarily offer themselves unto the society and fellowship thereof.—Acts ii. 41; 2 Cor. viii. 5.

EXPLICATION. — The means appointed by our Lord Jesus Christ for the continuance and increase of the church are either *preparatory* unto it or *instrumentally efficient of it*. The principal means subservient or *preparatory* unto the continuance and increase of the church is the preaching of the word to the conviction, illumination, and conversion of sinners, whereby they may be made meet to become living stones in this spiritual building, and members of the mystical body of Christ. And this is done either ordinarily, in the assemblies of the church, towards such as come in unto them and attend to the word dispensed according to the appointment of Christ amongst them, — 1 Cor. xiv. 24, 25, "If there come in one that believeth not, or one unlearned, he is convinced of all, he is judged of all: and thus are the secrets of his heart made manifest; and so falling down on his face he will worship God," — or occasionally, amongst the men of the world, Acts viii. 4.

Secondly, The *instrumentally efficient cause* is that which is expressed in the answer, — namely, the adding in due order unto it such as, being effectually called unto the obedience of the faith and profession of the gospel, do voluntarily, out of conviction of their duty and resolution to walk in subjection to all the ordinances and commands of Christ, offer themselves to the society and fellowship thereof, whereby they may be laid in this spiritual building as the stones were in the temple of old, which were hewed and fitted elsewhere.

Q. 48 *What is required of them who desire to join themselves unto the church?*

A. ªThat they be free from blame and offence in the world; ᵇthat they be instructed in the saving truths and mysteries of the gospel; ᶜsound in the faith; ᵈthat, the Lord having called them unto faith, repentance, and newness of life by Jesus Christ, they give up themselves to be saved by him, and to obey him in all things; and, therefore, ᵉare willing and ready, through his grace, to walk in subjection to all his commands, and in the observation of all his laws and institutions, notwithstanding any difficulties, oppositions, or persecutions, which they meet withal.—ªPhil. i. 10, ii. 15; 1 Cor. x. 32; 1 Thess. ii. 11, 12; Titus ii. 10.—ᵇJohn vi. 45; Acts xxvi. 18; 1 Pet. ii. 9; 2 Cor. iv. 3, 4, 6.—ᶜ1 Tim. i. 19, 20; 2 Tim. iv. 3, 4; Titus i. 13; Jude 3.—ᵈEph. iv. 20–24.—ᵉ2 Cor. viii. 5.

Q. 49 *What is the duty of the elders of the church towards persons desiring to be admitted unto the fellowship of the church?*

A. ªTo discern and judge by the rule of truth, applied in love, between sincere professors and hypocritical pretenders; ᵇto influence, direct, comfort, and encourage in the way, such as they judge to love the Lord Jesus in sincerity; ᶜto propose and recommend them unto the whole church, with prayers and supplications to God for them; ᵈto admit them, being approved, into the order and fellowship of the gospel in the church.—ªActs viii. 20, 23; Titus i. 10; Rev. ii. 2; Jer. xv. 19.—ᵇActs xviii.

26; 1 Thess. ii. 7, 8, 11.—ᶜActs ix. 27, 28.—ᵈRom. xiv. 1.

Q. 50 *What is the duty of the whole church in reference unto such persons?*

A. To consider them in love and meekness, according as their condition is known, reported, or testified unto them; to approve of and rejoice in the grace of God in them; and to receive them in love without dissimulation.—1 Cor. xiii.

EXPLICATION. — What in general is required, unto the fitting of any persons to be members of a visible church of Christ, was before declared; and that is that which the Lord Jesus hath made the indispensable condition of entering into his kingdom, — namely, of being "born again," John iii. 3, 5. This work, being secret, hidden, and invisible, the church cannot judge of directly and in its own form or nature, but in the means, effects, and consequents of it; which are to be testified unto it, concerning them who are to be admitted unto its fellowship and communion. It is required, therefore, of them, —

First, That they be of a conversation free from blame in the world; for whereas one end of the gathering of churches is to hold forth and express the holiness of the doctrine of Christ, and the power of his grace in turning men from all ungodliness unto sobriety, righteousness, and honesty, it is required of them that are admitted into them that they answer this end. And this the principle of grace, which is communicated unto them that believe, will effect and produce; for although it doth not follow that every one who hath attained an unblamable honesty in this world is inwardly quickened with a true principle of saving grace, yet it doth that they who are endowed with that principle will be so unblamable. And although they may on other accounts be evil spoken of, yet their good conversation in Christ will justify itself.

Secondly, Competent knowledge in the mysteries of the gospel is another means whereby the great qualification inquired after is testified unto the church; for as without this no privilege of the gospel can be profitably made use of, nor any duty of it rightly performed, so saving light is of the essence of conversion, and doth inseparably accompany it: 2 Cor. iv. 6, "God, who commanded the light to shine out of darkness, hath shined in our hearts, to give the light of the knowledge of the glory of God in the face of Jesus Christ." Where this is wanting, it is impossible for any person to evidence that he is delivered from that blindness, darkness, and ignorance, which all men are under the power of in the state of nature. Such a measure, then, of light and knowledge, as whereby men are enabled to apprehend aright of the person and offices of Christ, of the nature of his mediation, the benefits thereof, and the obedience that he requires at the hands of his disciples, is expected in them who desire to be admitted into the fellowship of the church.

Thirdly, Hereunto is to be added the soundness in the faith; for the unity of faith is the foundation of love and all the duties thereof, which in an especial manner are to be performed towards the church, called, therefore, "The household of faith." There is among the members of the church "one faith," Eph. iv. 5; the "common faith," [Titus i. 4]; the "faith once delivered unto the saints," Jude 3; which is the "sound doctrine," 1 Tim. i. 10, which those that will not endure must be turned from, 2 Tim. iii. 5; the "faithful word," that is to be "held fast," Titus i. 9, 1 Tim. i. 19, and which we are to be "sound in," Titus i. 13; contained in a "form of sound words," as to the profession of it, 2 Tim. i. 13. And this soundness in the unity of faith, as it should be improved unto oneness of mind and oneness of accord in all the things of God, Phil. ii. 2, though it may admit of some different apprehensions in some things, wherein some may have more clear and distinct discoveries of the mind and will of God than others, which hinders not but that all may walk according to the same rule, Phil. iii. 15, 16; so it is principally to be regarded in the fundamental truths of the gospel, in and by the faith whereof the church holdeth on the head, Jesus Christ, Col. ii. 19; and in the fundamental principles of gospel worship, the joint celebration whereof is the next end of the gathering the church: for without a consent of mind and accord herein, no duty can be performed unto the edification, nor the peace of the church be preserved. And these principles are those which we have explained.

Fourthly, It is required that these things be testified by them unto the church, with the acknowledgment of the work of God's grace towards them, and their resolution, through the power of the same grace, to cleave unto the Lord Christ with full purpose of heart, and to live in all holy obedience unto him. They come to the church as disciples of Christ, professing that they have learnt the truth as it is in Jesus: which what it infers the apostle teacheth at large, Eph. iv. 20–24; see also Acts xi. 23, xiv. 22. And this by themselves [is] to be testified unto the church:—

1. That they may be received in love without

dissimulation, as real partakers in the same faith, hope, and salvation with themselves, as living members of the mystical body of Christ.

2. That on all ensuing occasions they may be minded of their own profession and engagements, to stir them up thereby unto faithfulness, steadfastness, and perseverance. Hereupon are the elders of the church to judge by the rule of truth, in love and meekness, concerning their condition and meetness to be laid as living stones in the house of God; so as that they may, —

(1.) Reject false, hypocritical pretenders, if in or by any means their hypocrisy be discovered unto them, Acts viii. 20–23; Titus i. 10; Jer. xv. 19.

(2.) That they may direct and encourage in the way such as appear to be sincere, instructing them principally in the nature of the way whereinto they are engaging, the duties, dangers, and benefits of it, Acts xviii. 26, xiv. 22; 1 Cor. iii. 22, 23.

(3.) To propose them, their condition, their desires, their resolutions, unto the church, after their own expressions of them, to be considered of in love and meekness, Acts ix. 26, 27. Whereupon those that are approved do give up themselves unto the Lord, to walk in the observation of all his commands and ordinances; and to the church for the Lord's sake, 2 Cor. viii. 5, abiding in the fellowship thereof, whereunto they are admitted, Acts ii. 41, 42.

Q. 51 *Wherein doth the especial form of a particular church, whereby it becomes such, and is distinguished as such from all others, consist?*

A. In the special consent and agreement of all the members of it to walk together in the observation of the same ordinances numerically; hence its constitution and distinction from other churches doth proceed.—Exod. xix. 5, 8, xxiv. 3, 7; Deut. xxvi. 17; 2 Cor. viii. 5; Acts xiv. 23, xx. 28; Heb. xiii. 17.

EXPLICATION. — It hath been before declared what especial agreement or covenant there ought to be among all the members of the same church, to walk together in a due subjection unto and observance of all the institutions of the Lord Christ. And this is that which gives it its special *form* and distinction from all other churches. In the general nature of a church, all churches do agree and equally partake. There is the same law of the constitution of them all; they have all the same rule of obedience, all the same Head, the same end; all carry it on by the observation of the same ordinances in *kind*. Now, besides these things, which belong unto the nature of a church in general, and wherein they all equally participate, they must also have each one its proper difference, that which doth distinguish it from all other churches; and this gives it its special form as such. Now, this cannot consist in any thing that is accidental, occasional, or extrinsical unto it, such as is cohabitation (which yet the church may have respect unto, for conveniency and furthering of its edification); nor in any civil or political disposal of its members into civil societies for civil ends, which is extrinsical to all its concernments as a church; nor doth it consist in the relation of that church to its present officers, which may be removed or taken away without the dissolution of the form or being of the church: but it consisteth, as was said, in the agreement or covenant before mentioned. For, —

First, This is that which constitutes them a *distinct body*, different from others; for thereby, and no otherwise, do they coalesce into a society, according to the laws of their constitution and appointment.

Secondly, This gives them their *especial relation* unto their own elders, rulers, or guides, who watch over them as so associated by their own consent, according unto the command of Christ. And, —

Thirdly, From hence they have their mutual especial relation unto one another; which is the ground of the especial exercise of all church duties whatsoever.

Q. 52 *Wherein consists the duty of any church of Christ towards other churches?*

A. ᵃIn walking circumspectly, so as to give them no offence; ᵇin prayer for their peace and prosperity; ᶜin communicating supplies to their wants according to ability; ᵈin receiving with love and readiness the members of them into fellowship, in the celebration of the ordinances of the gospel, as occasion shall be; ᵉin desiring and making use of their counsel and advice in such cases of doubt and difficulty as may arise among them; ᶠin joining with them to express their communion in the same doctrine of faith.—ᵃ1 Cor. x. 32.—ᵇPs. cxxii. 6; Eph. vi. 18; 1 Tim. ii. 1.—ᶜ2 Cor. viii. 1–15; Acts xi. 29, 30; Rom. xv. 26, 27.—ᵈRom. xvi. 1, 2; 3 John 8, 9.—ᵉActs xv. 2, 6.—ᶠ1 Tim. iii. 15.

EXPLICATION. — Churches being gathered and settled according to the mind of Christ, ought to preserve a mutual holy communion among themselves, and to exercise it in the discharge of those duties whereby their mutual good and edification may be promoted; for whereas they are all united under one head, the Lord Christ, Eph. i. 22, 23, in the same faith and order, chap. iv. 5, and do walk by the same rule, they stand in such a relation one to another as is the ground of the communion spoken of. Now, the principal ways whereby they exercise this communion are the acts and duties enumerated in the answer to this question; as, —

First, Careful walking, so as to give no offence unto one another; which, although it be a moral duty in reference unto all, yet therein especial regard is to be had unto other churches of Christ, that they be not in any thing grieved or tempted: 1 Cor. x. 32, "Give none offence, neither to the Jews, nor to the Gentiles, nor to the church of God."

Secondly, In constant prayer for the peace, welfare, edification, and prosperity one of another, Rom. i. 9; Col. i. 9; Eph. vi. 18. And this because of the special concernment of the name and glory of our Lord Jesus Christ in their welfare.

Thirdly, In communicating of supplies for their relief according unto their ability, in case of the outward wants, straits, dangers, or necessities of any of them. — Acts xi. 29, 30; Rom. xv. 26, 27; 2 Cor. viii. 1–15.

Fourthly, The receiving of the members of other churches to communion, in the celebration of church-ordinances, is another way whereby this communion of churches is exercised, Rom. xvi. 1, 2; 3 John 8, 9; for whereas the personal right of such persons unto the ordinances of the church, and their orderly walking in the observation of the commands of Christ, are known by the testimony of the church whereof they are members, they may, without farther inquiry or satisfaction given, be looked on "pro tempore" as members of the church wherein they desire fellowship and participation of the ordinances of Christ.

Fifthly, In desiring or making use of the counsel and advice of one another, in such cases of doubt and difficulty, whether *doctrinal* or *practical*, as may arise in any of them, Acts xv. 2, 6. And from hence it follows, that in case any church, either by error in doctrine, or precipitation, or mistake in other administrations, do give offence unto other churches, those other churches may require an account from them, admonish them of their faults, and withhold communion from them in case they persist in the error of their way; and that because in their difficulties, and before their miscarriages, they were bound to have desired the advice, counsel, and assistance of those other churches, which being neglected by them, the other are to recover the end of it unto their utmost ability, Gal. ii. 6–11. And hence, also, it follows that those that are rightly and justly censured in any church ought to be rejected by all churches whatever; both because of their mutual communion, and because it is and ought to be presumed, until the contrary be made to appear, that, in case there had been any difficulty or doubt in the procedure of the church, they would have taken the advice of those churches, with whom they were obliged to consult.

Lastly, Whereas the churches have all of them one *common faith*, and are all obliged to hold forth and declare it to all men as they have opportunity, 1 Tim. iii. 15, to testify this their mutual communion, their interest in the same faith and hope, for the more open declaration and proposition of the truths of the gospel which they profess, and for the vindication both of the truth and themselves from false charges and imputations, they may, and, if God give opportunity, ought to join together in declaring and testifying their joint consent and fellowship in the same doctrine of faith, expressed in a "form of sound words."

Q. 53 *What are the ends of all this dispensation and order of things in the church?*

A. The glory of God, the honour of Jesus Christ the mediator, the furtherance of the gospel, the edification and consolation of believers here, with their eternal salvation hereafter.—Rev. iv. 9–11, v. 12, 13; 1 Cor. iii. 22, 23; Eph. iv. 11–16.

www.ingramcontent.com/pod-product-compliance
Lightning Source LLC
Chambersburg PA
CBHW030333100526
44592CB00010B/677